GRAPHIC BIOGRAPHIES

FLORENCE NIGHTINGALE

Lady with the Lamp

by Trina Robbins

illustrated by Anne Timmons

Consultant:
Laurie K. Glass, RN, PhD, FAAN
Professor Emerita
University of Wisconsin-Milwaukee

Capstone

Mankato, Minnesota

Graphic Library is published by Capstone Press,
151 Good Counsel Drive, P.O. Box 669, Mankato, Minnesota 56002.
www.capstonepress.com

Printed in the United States of America

1 2 3 4 5 6 12 11 10 09 08 07

Library of Congress Cataloging-in-Publication Data
Robbins, Trina.
Florence Nightingale: lady with the lamp / by Trina Robbins; illustrated by Anne Timmons.
p. cm. —(Graphic library. Graphic biographies)
Summary: "In graphic novel format, tells the life story of Florence Nightingale, the English nurse who reformed military hospitals during the Crimean War and became the founder of modern nursing"—Provided by publisher.
Includes bibliographical references and index.
ISBN-13: 978-0-7368-6850-1 (hardcover)
ISBN-10: 0-7368-6850-X (hardcover)
ISBN-13: 978-0-7368-7902-6 (softcover pbk.)
ISBN-10: 0-7368-7902-1 (softcover pbk.)
1. Nightingale, Florence, 1820–1910—Juvenile literature. 2. Nurses—England—Biography—Juvenile literature. I. Timmons, Anne, ill. II. Title. III. Series.
RT37.N5R63 2007
610.73092—dc22
[B] 2006025905

Designer
Alison Thiele

Production Designers
Renée Doyle and Kim Brown

Colorist
Brent Schoonover

Editor
Christine Peterson

Editor's note: Direct quotations from primary sources are indicated by a yellow background.

Direct quotations appear on the following pages:
Page 6, from an 1849 diary entry by Florence Nightingale as published in *Florence Nightingale: Mystic, Visionary, Healer* by Barbara Montgomery Dossey (Springhouse, Pa.: Springhouse Corporation, 2000).
Page 10, from an 1851 letter by Florence Nightingale, as published in *The Collected Works of Florence Nightingale*, edited by Lynn McDonald (Waterloo, Ontario, Canada: Wilfrid Laurier University Press, 2004).

TABLE OF CONTENTS

Chapter 1

A Life of Luxury

Florence Nightingale was born to a wealthy English family. Unlike most people in the 1800s, her father believed girls should be educated. William Nightingale taught French, history, and mathematics to young Florence and her sister, Parthenope.

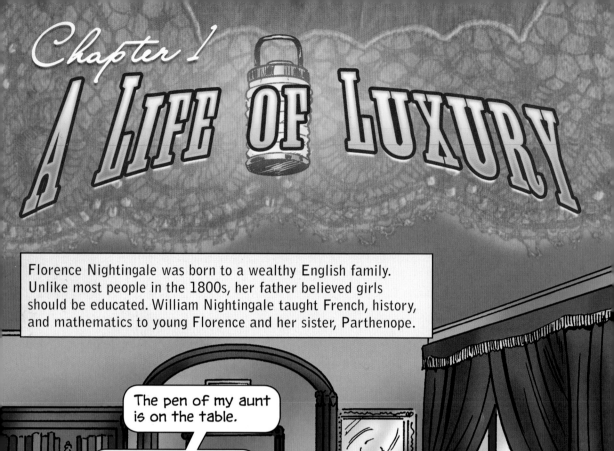

The pen of my aunt is on the table.

La plume de ma tante est sur la table.

Your French is improving, Florence.

Parthenope, pay attention. You need to learn this.

Why, Father? I'll have no use for French. I just want to find a good husband to marry.

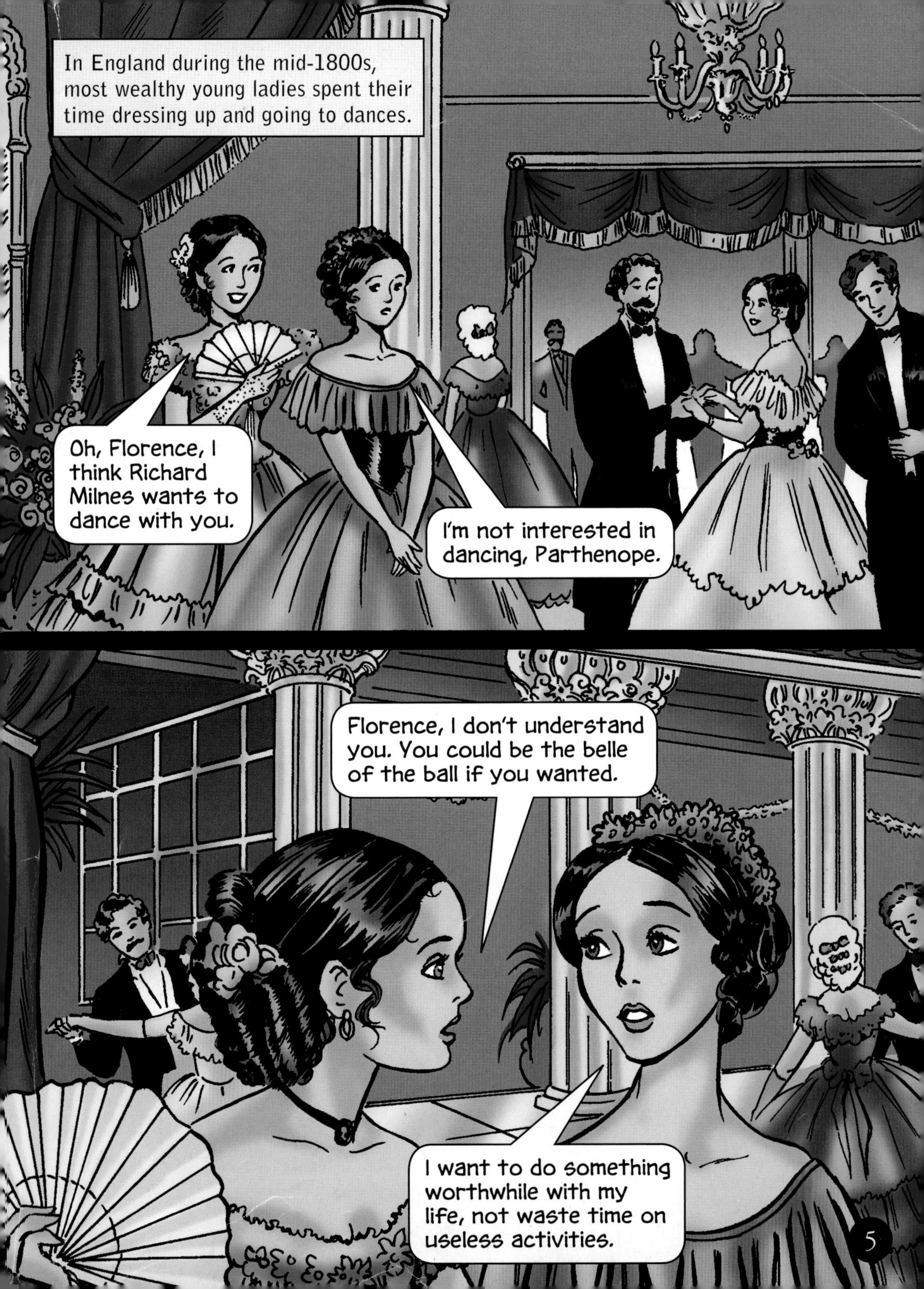
In England during the mid-1800s, most wealthy young ladies spent their time dressing up and going to dances.
Oh, Florence, I think Richard Milnes wants to dance with you.
I'm not interested in dancing, Parthenope.
Florence, I don't understand you. You could be the belle of the ball if you wanted.
I want to do something worthwhile with my life, not waste time on useless activities.

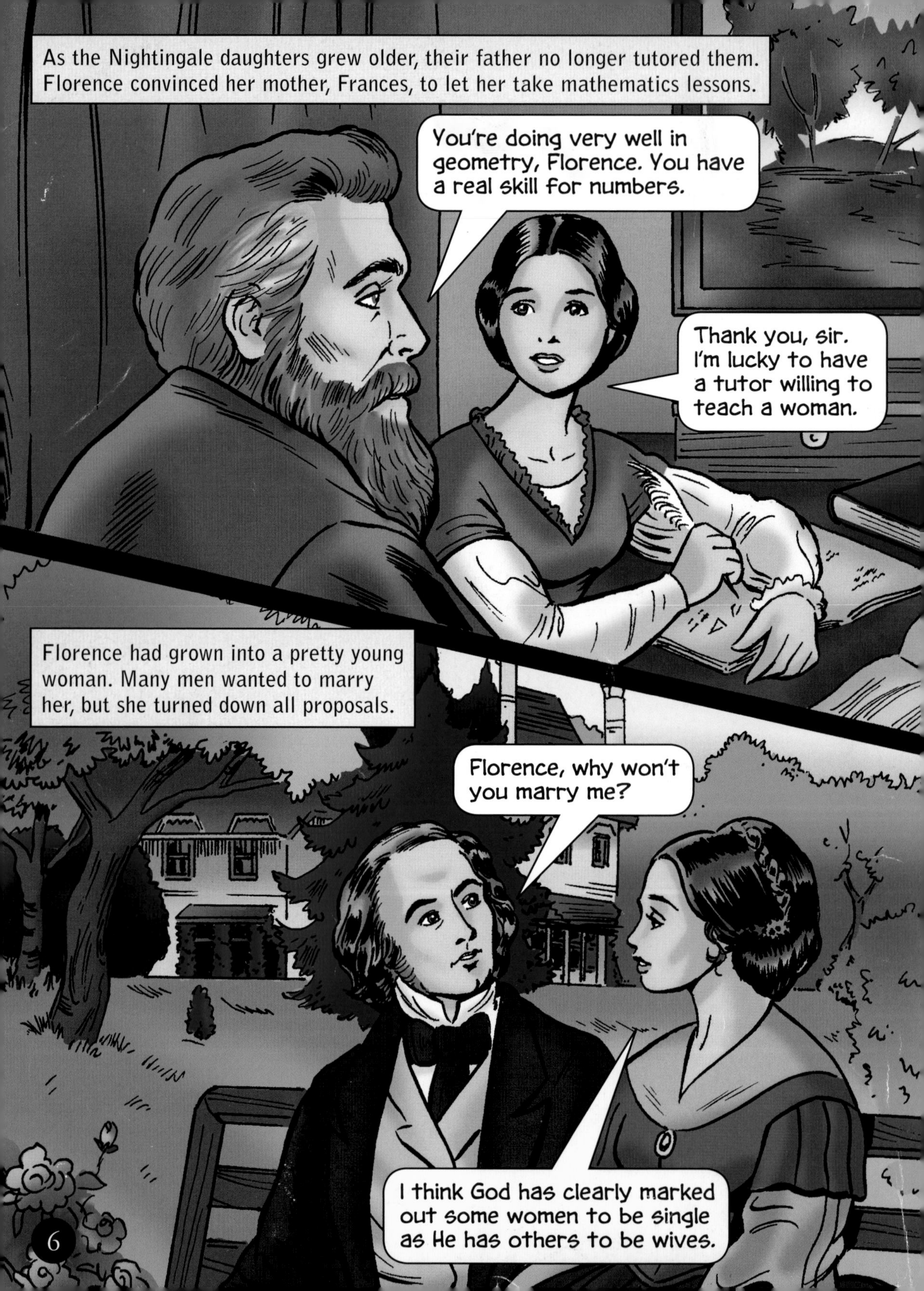

As the Nightingale daughters grew older, their father no longer tutored them. Florence convinced her mother, Frances, to let her take mathematics lessons.
You're doing very well in geometry, Florence. You have a real skill for numbers.
Thank you, sir. I'm lucky to have a tutor willing to teach a woman.
Florence had grown into a pretty young woman. Many men wanted to marry her, but she turned down all proposals.
Florence, why won't you marry me?
I think God has clearly marked out some women to be single as He has others to be wives.

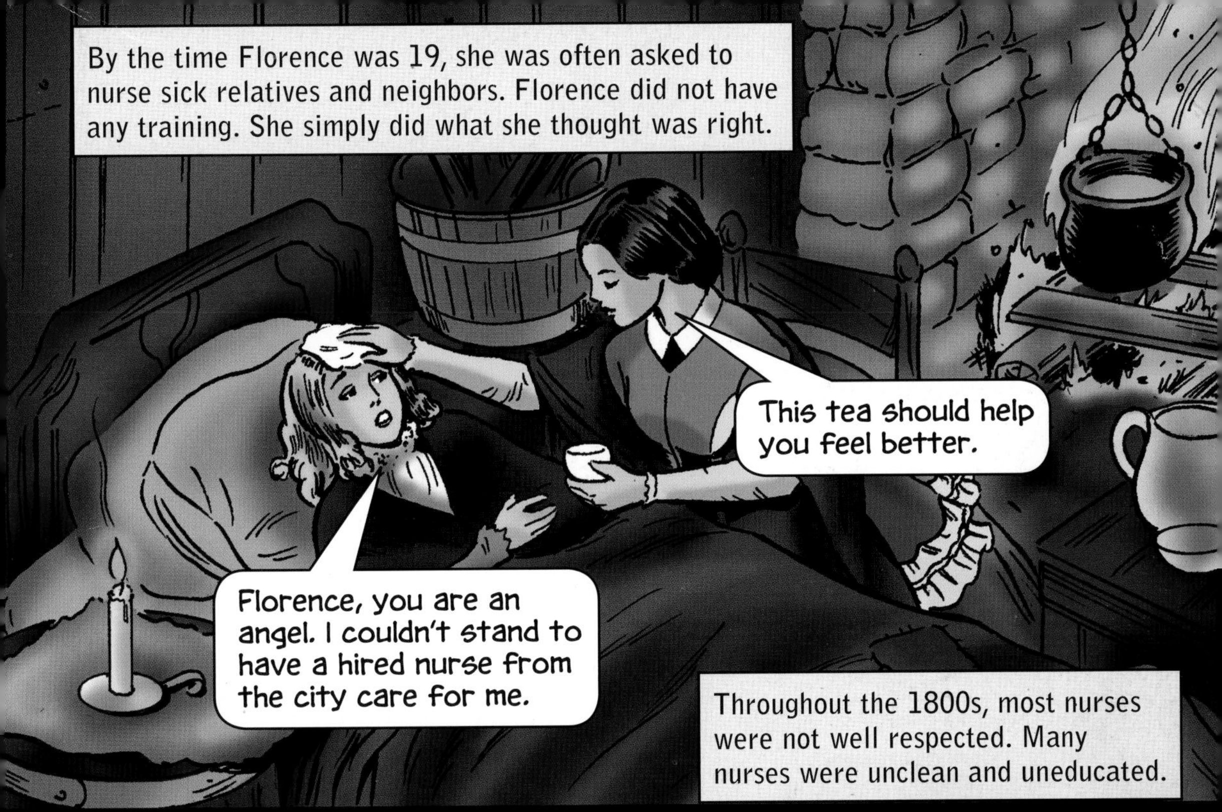
By the time Florence was 19, she was often asked to nurse sick relatives and neighbors. Florence did not have any training. She simply did what she thought was right.
This tea should help you feel better.
Florence, you are an angel. I couldn't stand to have a hired nurse from the city care for me.
Throughout the 1800s, most nurses were not well respected. Many nurses were unclean and uneducated.

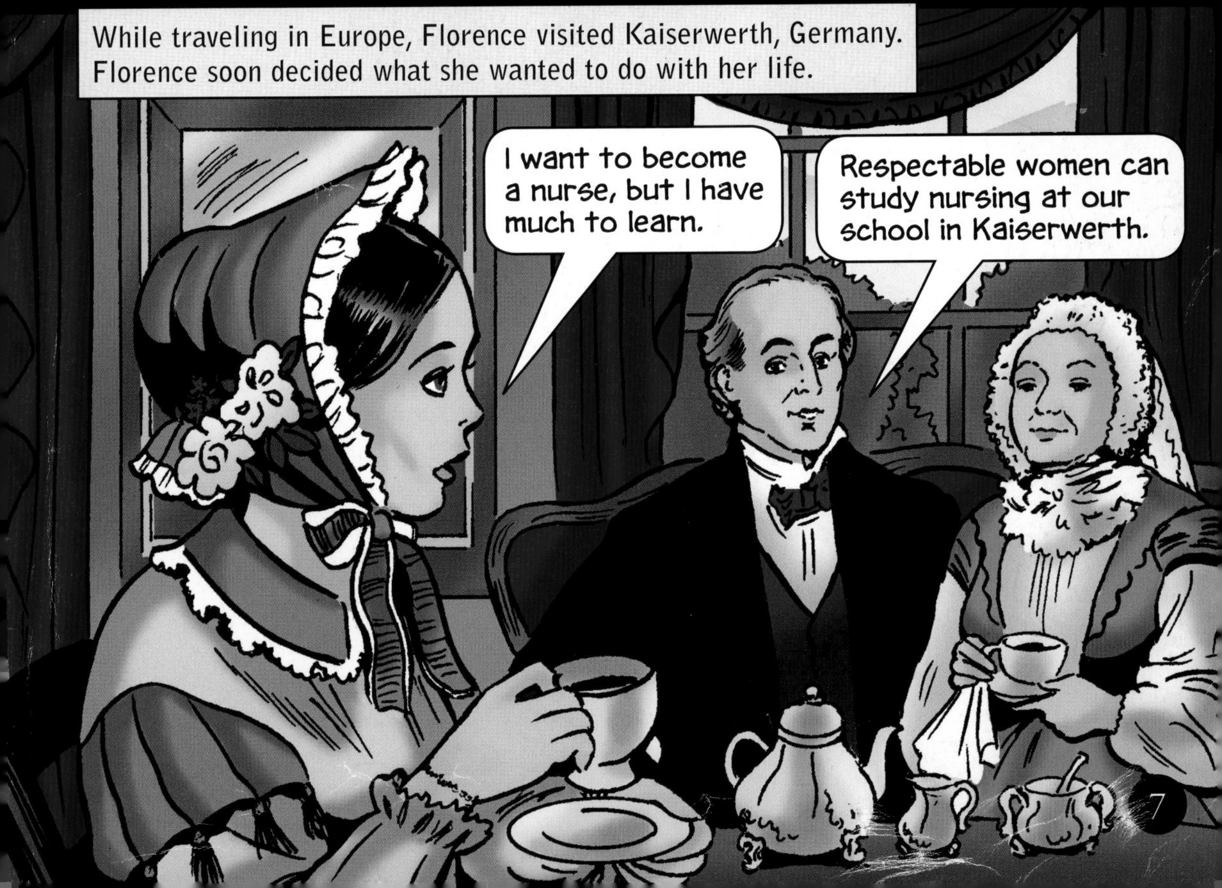
While traveling in Europe, Florence visited Kaiserwerth, Germany. Florence soon decided what she wanted to do with her life.
I want to become a nurse, but I have much to learn.
Respectable women can study nursing at our school in Kaiserwerth.

Chapter 2
A Call to Nursing

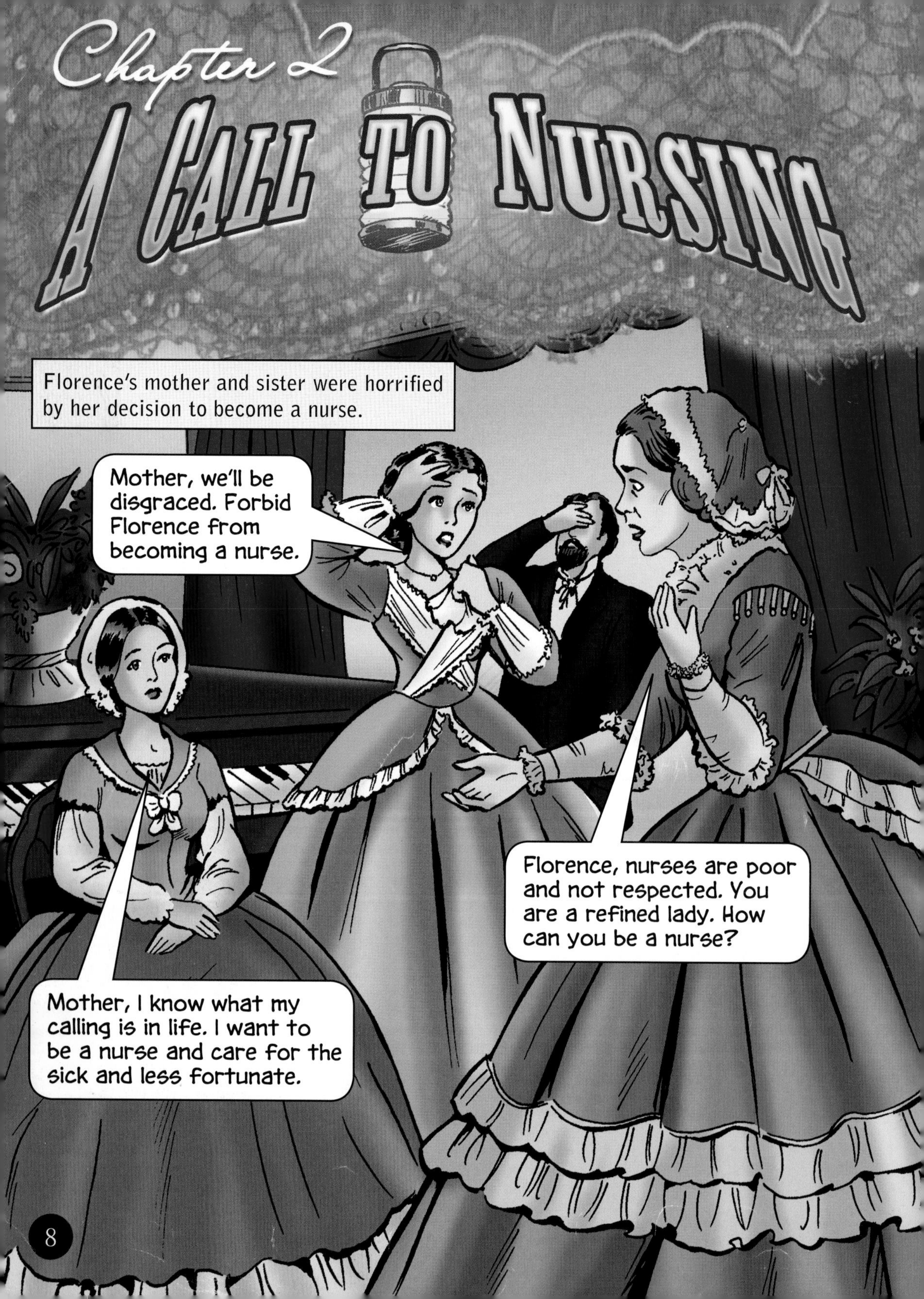
Florence's mother and sister were horrified by her decision to become a nurse.
Mother, we'll be disgraced. Forbid Florence from becoming a nurse.
Florence, nurses are poor and not respected. You are a refined lady. How can you be a nurse?
Mother, I know what my calling is in life. I want to be a nurse and care for the sick and less fortunate.

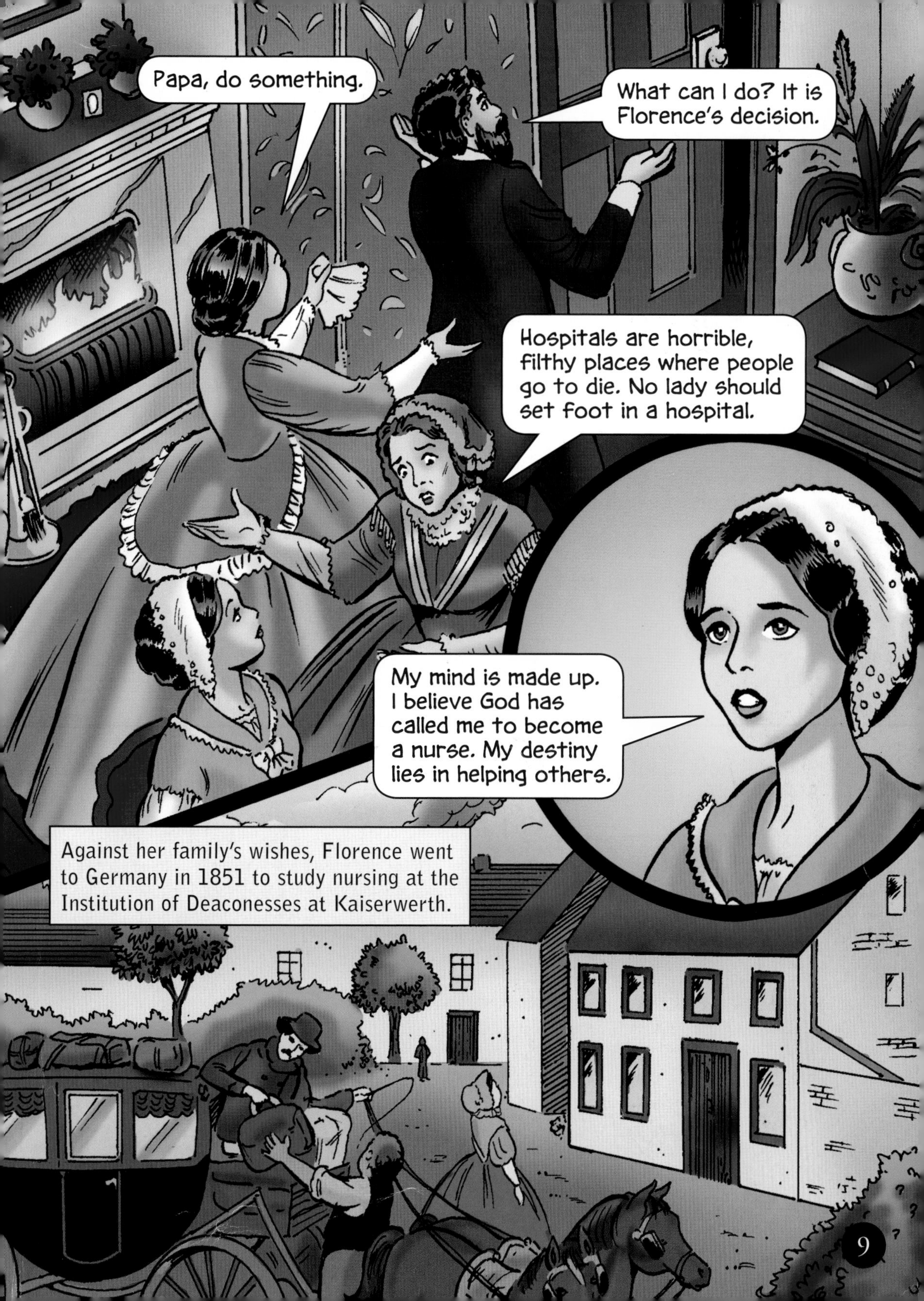
Papa, do something.
What can I do? It is Florence's decision.
Hospitals are horrible, filthy places where people go to die. No lady should set foot in a hospital.
My mind is made up. I believe God has called me to become a nurse. My destiny lies in helping others.
Against her family's wishes, Florence went to Germany in 1851 to study nursing at the Institution of Deaconesses at Kaiserwerth.

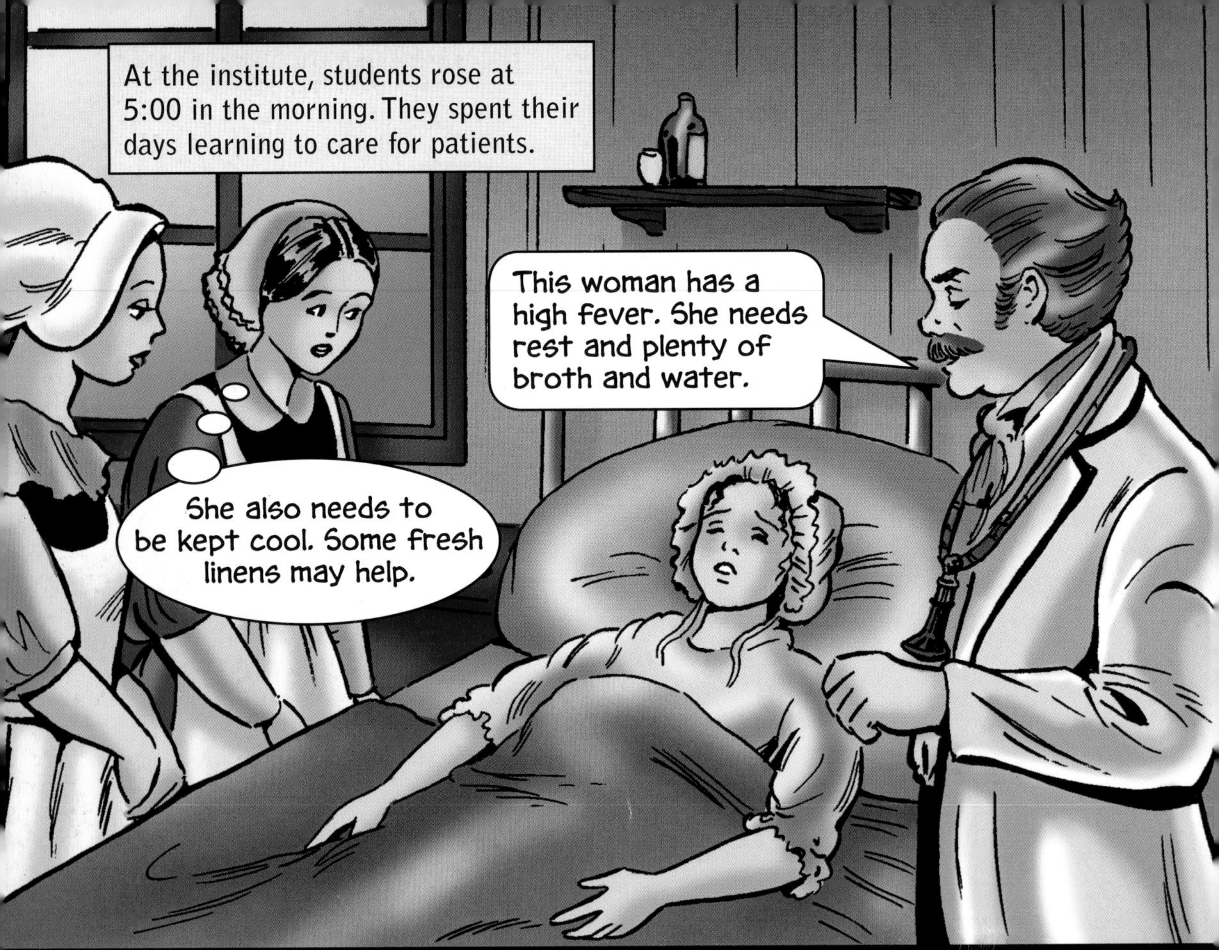
At the institute, students rose at 5:00 in the morning. They spent their days learning to care for patients.
This woman has a high fever. She needs rest and plenty of broth and water.
She also needs to be kept cool. Some fresh linens may help.

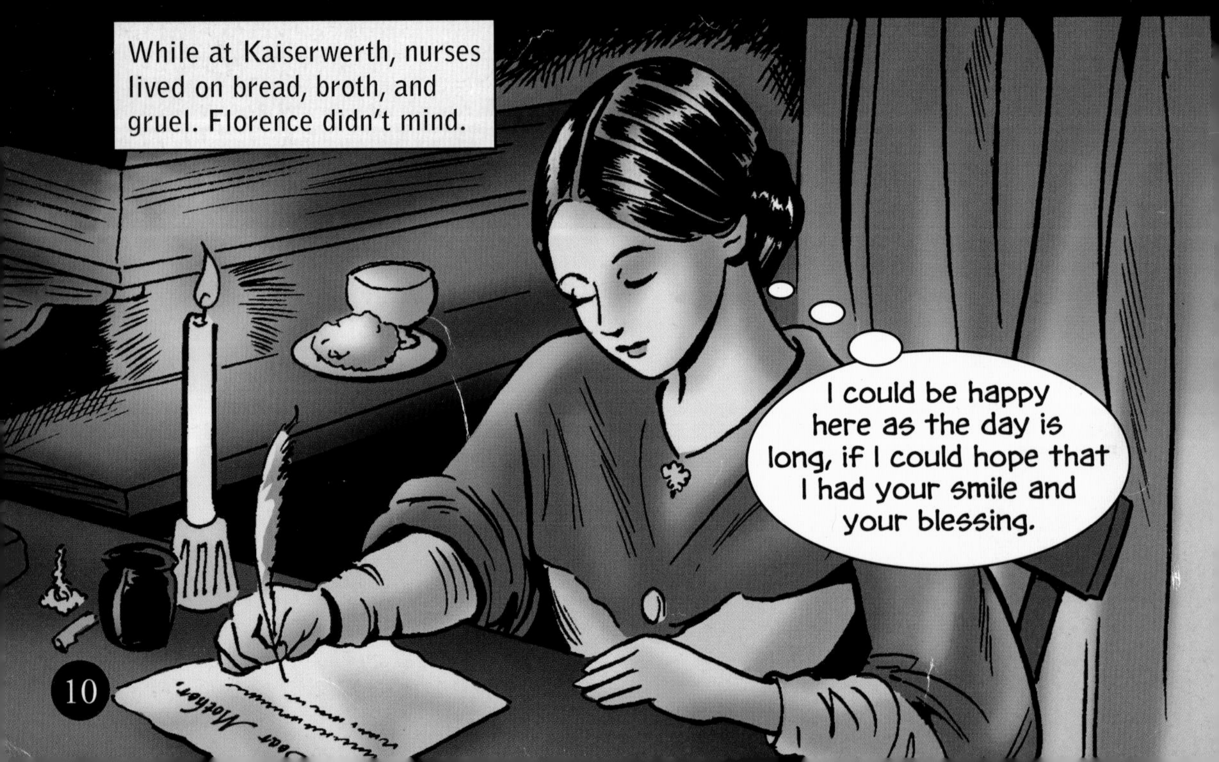
While at Kaiserwerth, nurses lived on bread, broth, and gruel. Florence didn't mind.
I could be happy here as the day is long, if I could hope that I had your smile and your blessing.
Dear Mother,

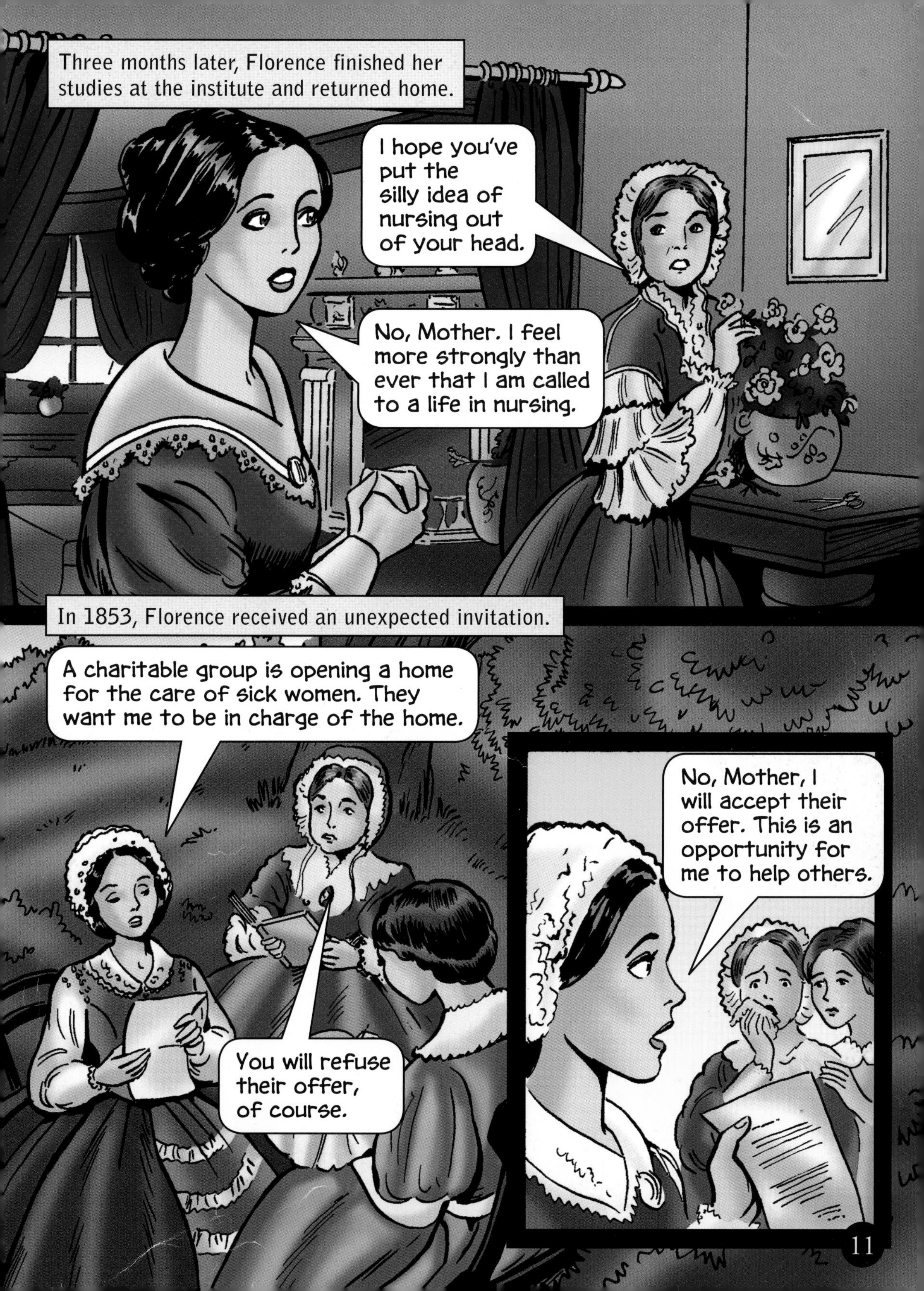
Three months later, Florence finished her studies at the institute and returned home.
I hope you've put the silly idea of nursing out of your head.
No, Mother. I feel more strongly than ever that I am called to a life in nursing.
In 1853, Florence received an unexpected invitation.
A charitable group is opening a home for the care of sick women. They want me to be in charge of the home.
You will refuse their offer, of course.
No, Mother, I will accept their offer. This is an opportunity for me to help others.

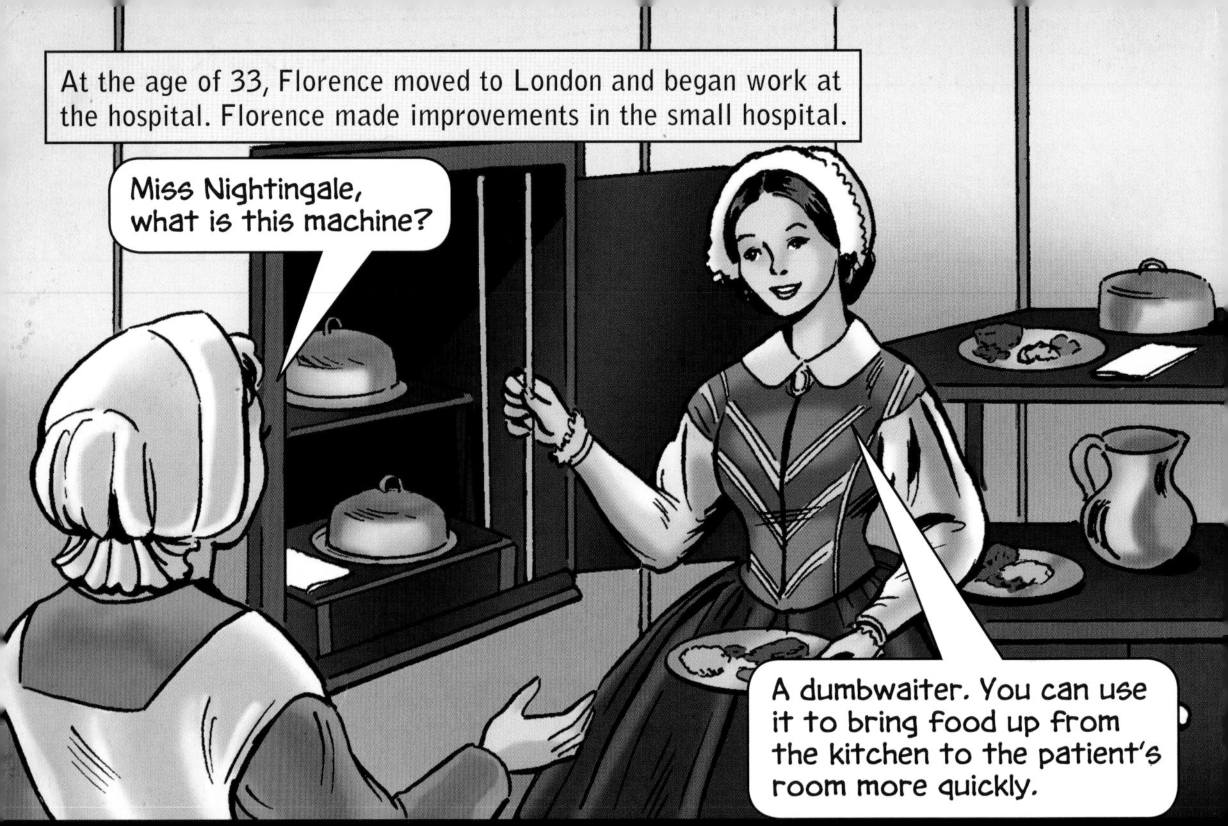
At the age of 33, Florence moved to London and began work at the hospital. Florence made improvements in the small hospital.
Miss Nightingale, what is this machine?
A dumbwaiter. You can use it to bring food up from the kitchen to the patient's room more quickly.

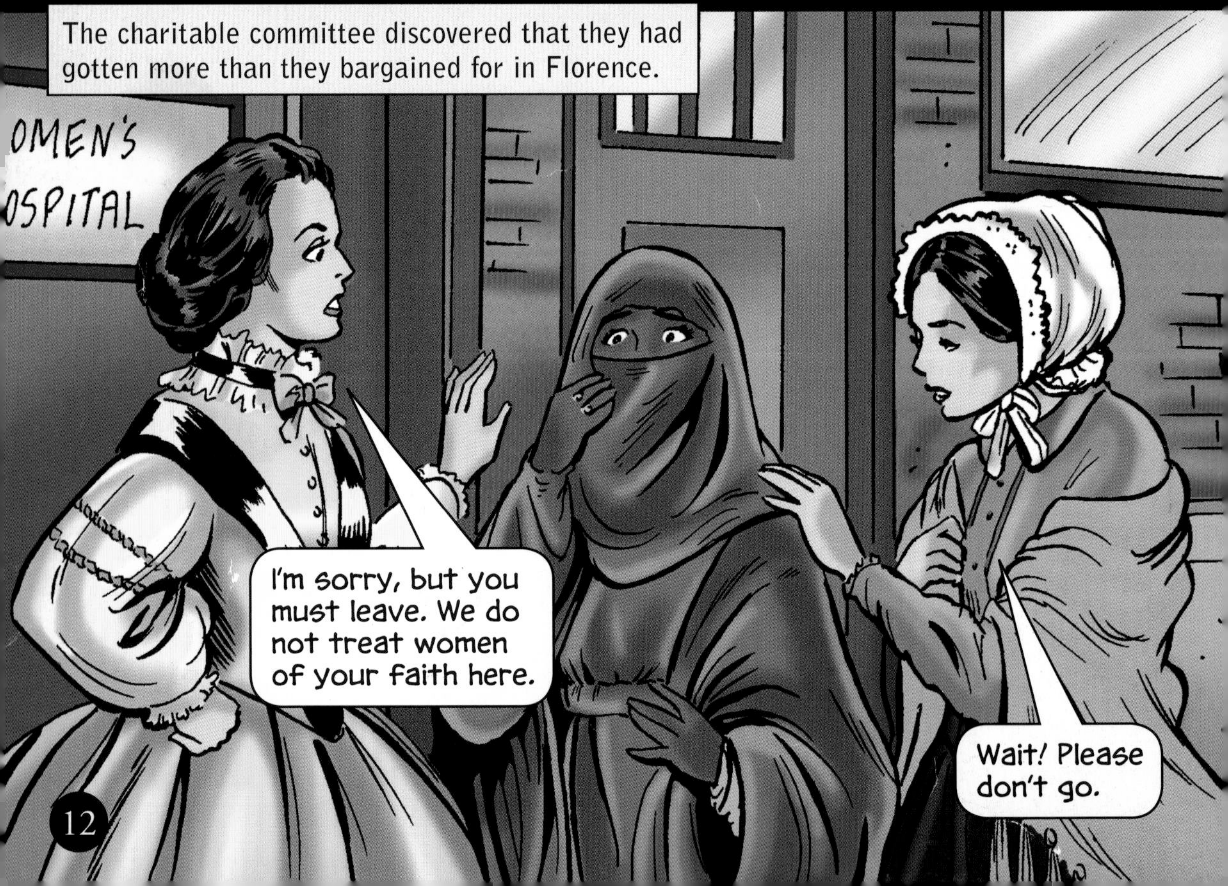
The charitable committee discovered that they had gotten more than they bargained for in Florence.
OMEN'S
OSPITAL
I'm sorry, but you must leave. We do not treat women of your faith here.
Wait! Please don't go.

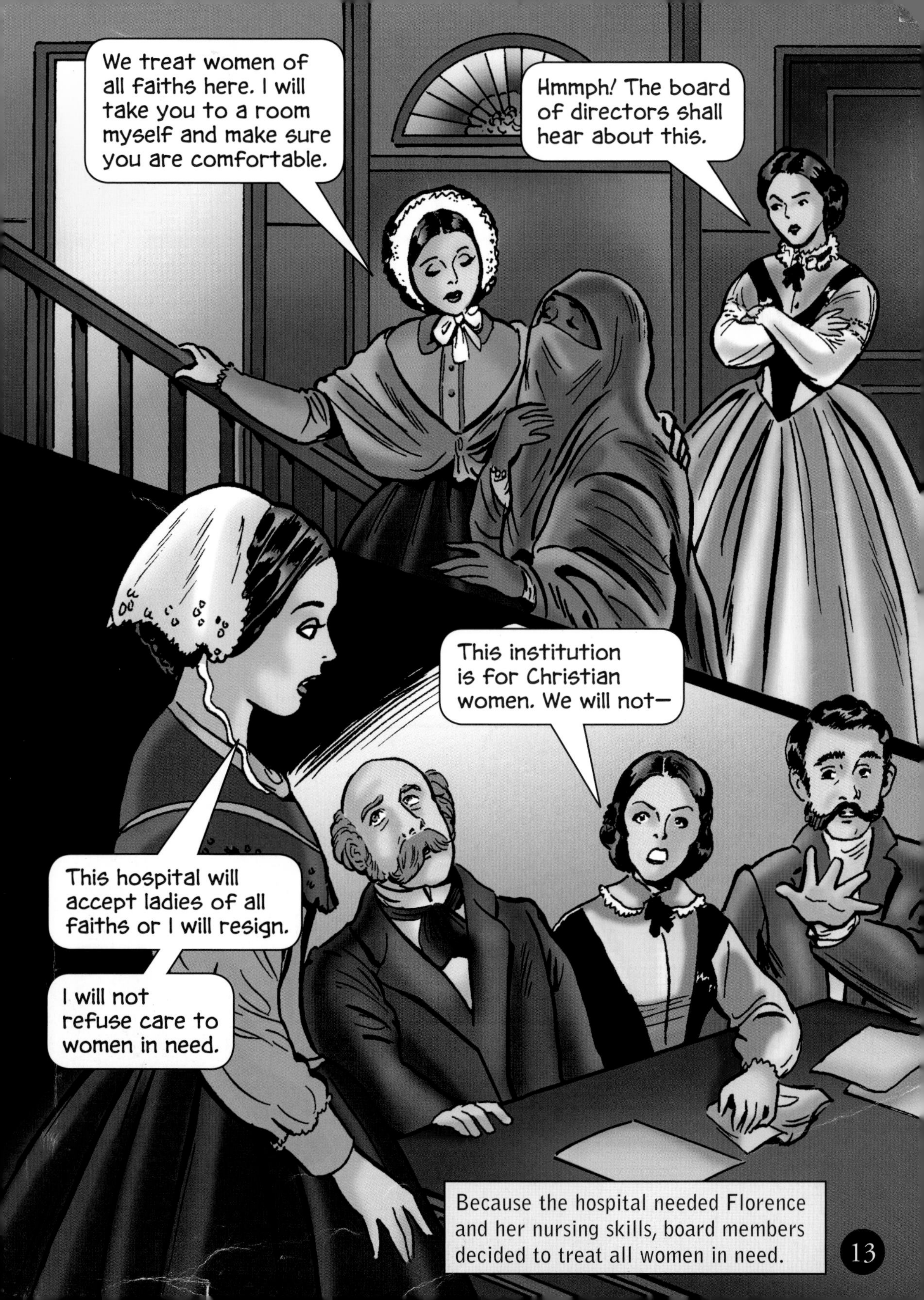

We treat women of all faiths here. I will take you to a room myself and make sure you are comfortable.
Hmmph! The board of directors shall hear about this.
This institution is for Christian women. We will not—
This hospital will accept ladies of all faiths or I will resign.
I will not refuse care to women in need.
Because the hospital needed Florence and her nursing skills, board members decided to treat all women in need.

Chapter 3
Florence Goes to War

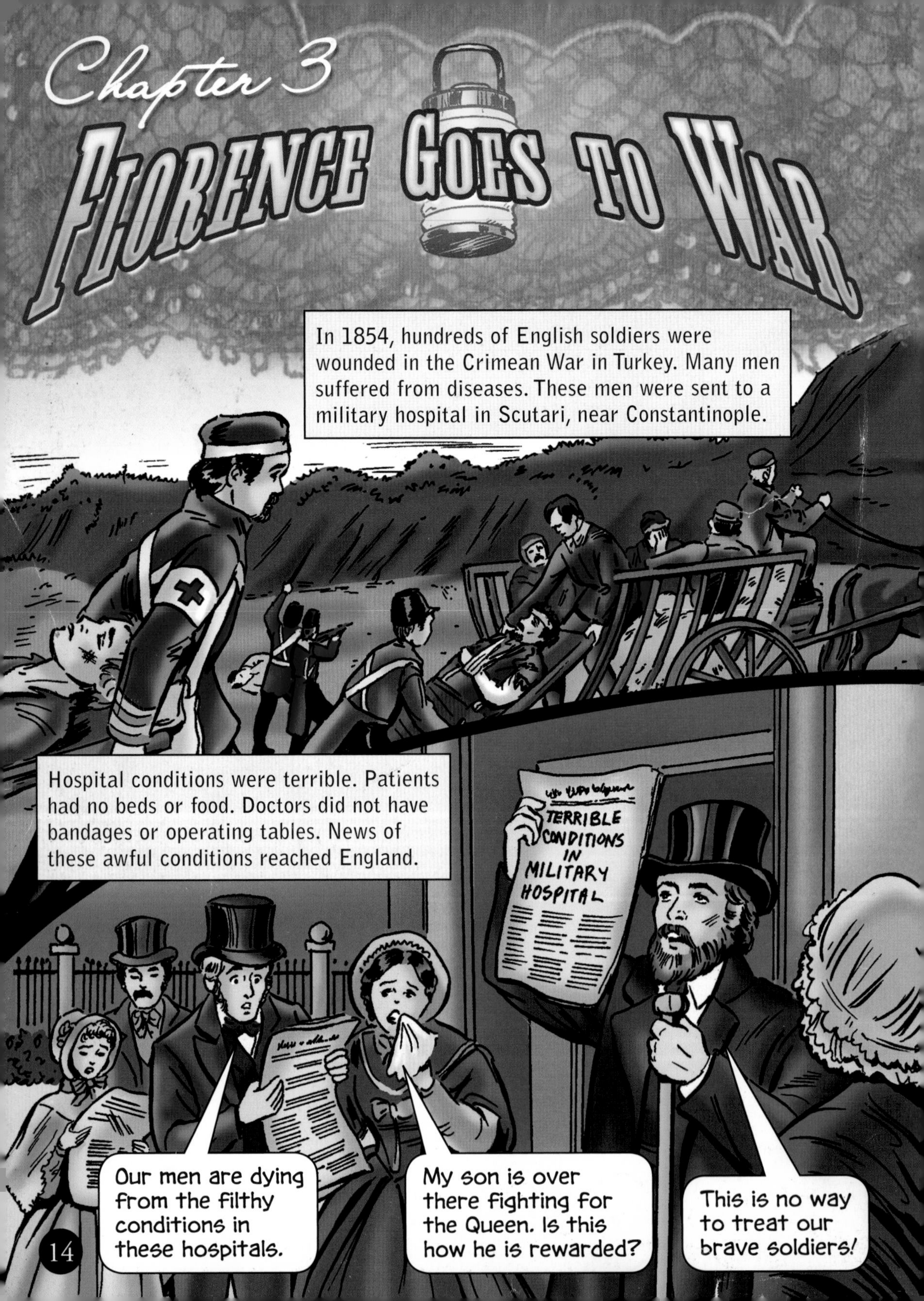
In 1854, hundreds of English soldiers were wounded in the Crimean War in Turkey. Many men suffered from diseases. These men were sent to a military hospital in Scutari, near Constantinople.
Hospital conditions were terrible. Patients had no beds or food. Doctors did not have bandages or operating tables. News of these awful conditions reached England.
TERRIBLE CONDITIONS IN MILITARY HOSPITAL
Our men are dying from the filthy conditions in these hospitals.
My son is over there fighting for the Queen. Is this how he is rewarded?
This is no way to treat our brave soldiers!

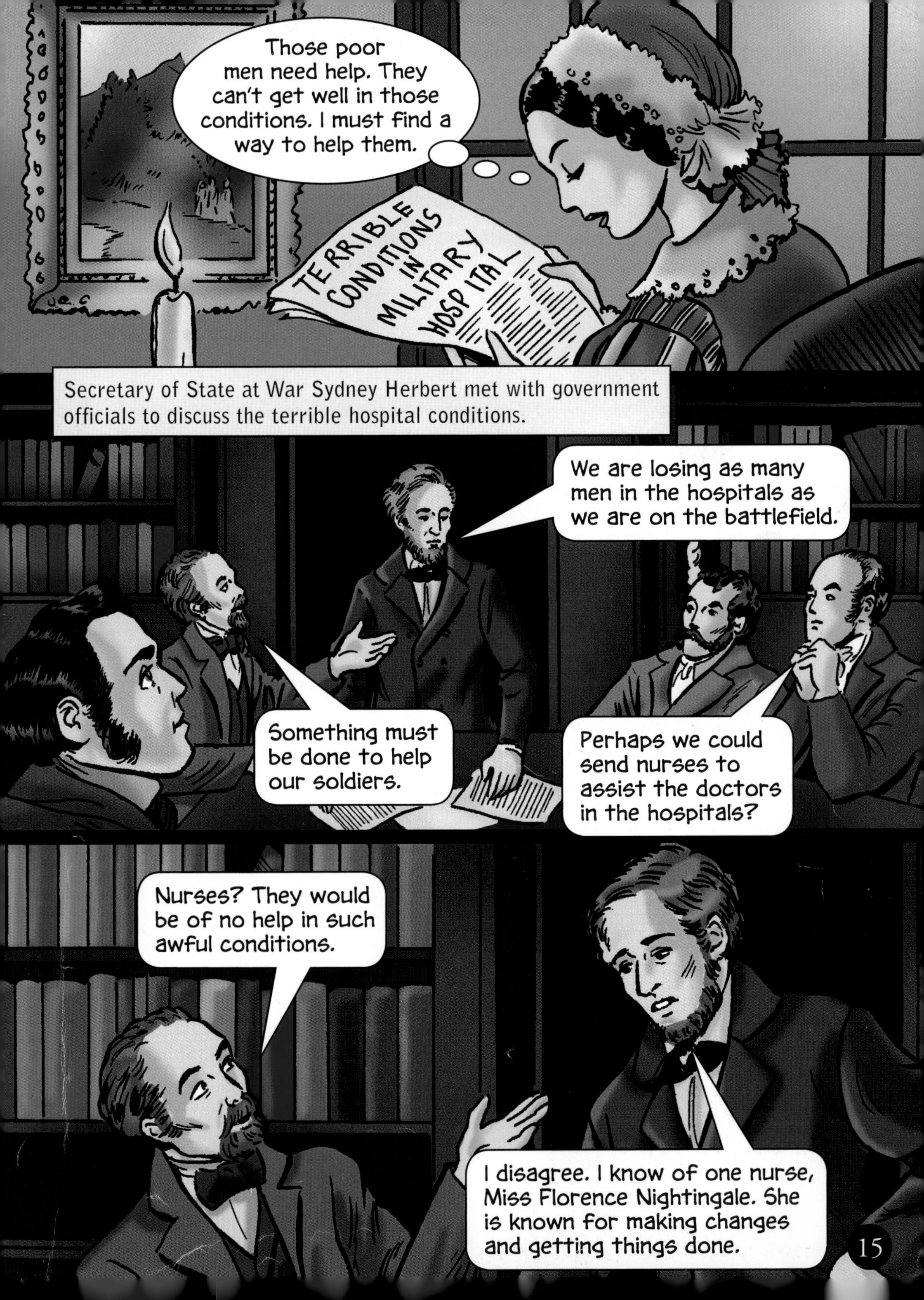
Those poor men need help. They can't get well in those conditions. I must find a way to help them.
TERRIBLE CONDITIONS IN MILITARY HOSPITAL
Secretary of State at War Sydney Herbert met with government officials to discuss the terrible hospital conditions.
We are losing as many men in the hospitals as we are on the battlefield.
Something must be done to help our soldiers.
Perhaps we could send nurses to assist the doctors in the hospitals?
Nurses? They would be of no help in such awful conditions.
I disagree. I know of one nurse, Miss Florence Nightingale. She is known for making changes and getting things done.

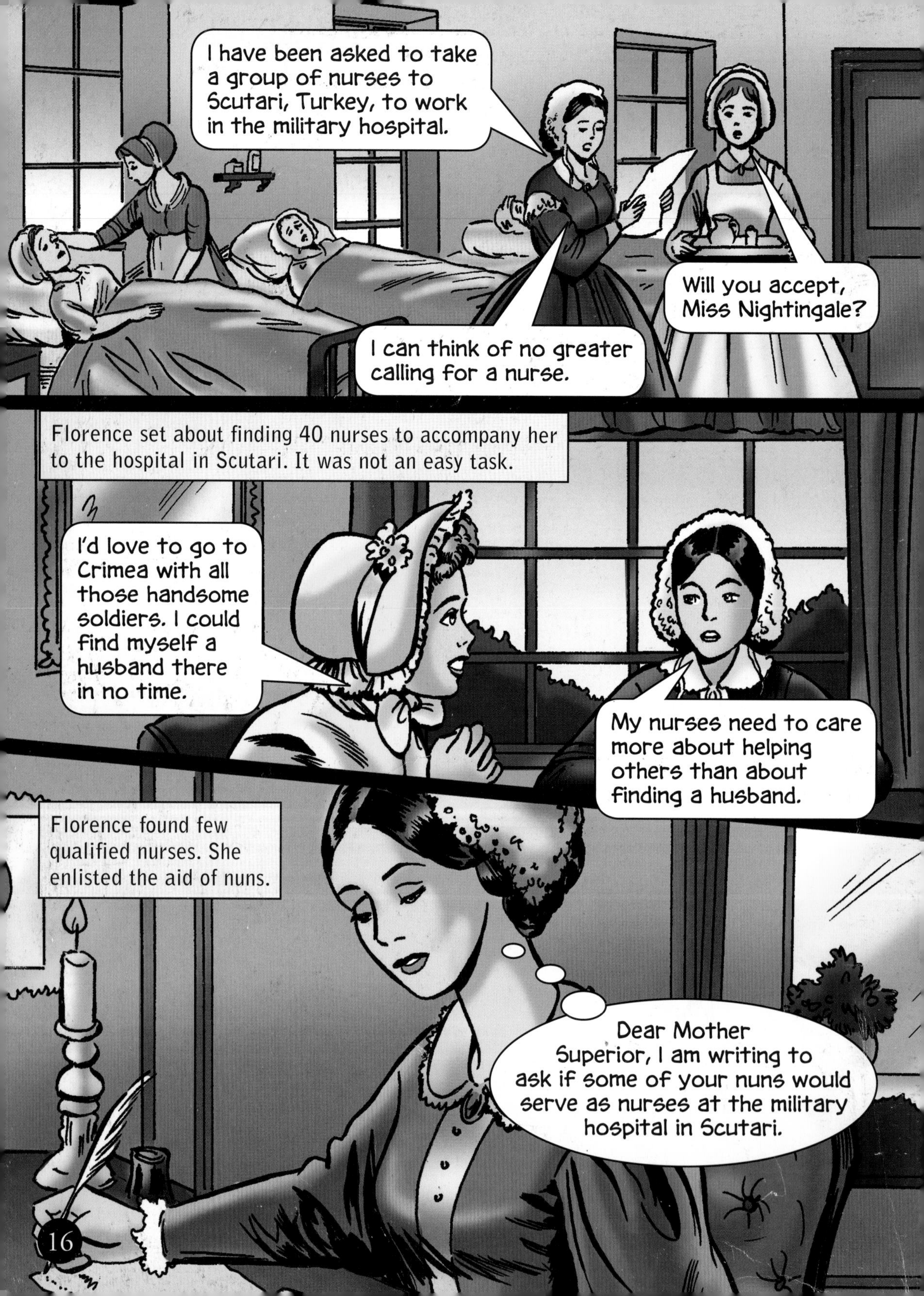
I have been asked to take a group of nurses to Scutari, Turkey, to work in the military hospital.
Will you accept, Miss Nightingale?
I can think of no greater calling for a nurse.
Florence set about finding 40 nurses to accompany her to the hospital in Scutari. It was not an easy task.
I'd love to go to Crimea with all those handsome soldiers. I could find myself a husband there in no time.
My nurses need to care more about helping others than about finding a husband.
Florence found few qualified nurses. She enlisted the aid of nuns.
Dear Mother Superior, I am writing to ask if some of your nuns would serve as nurses at the military hospital in Scutari.

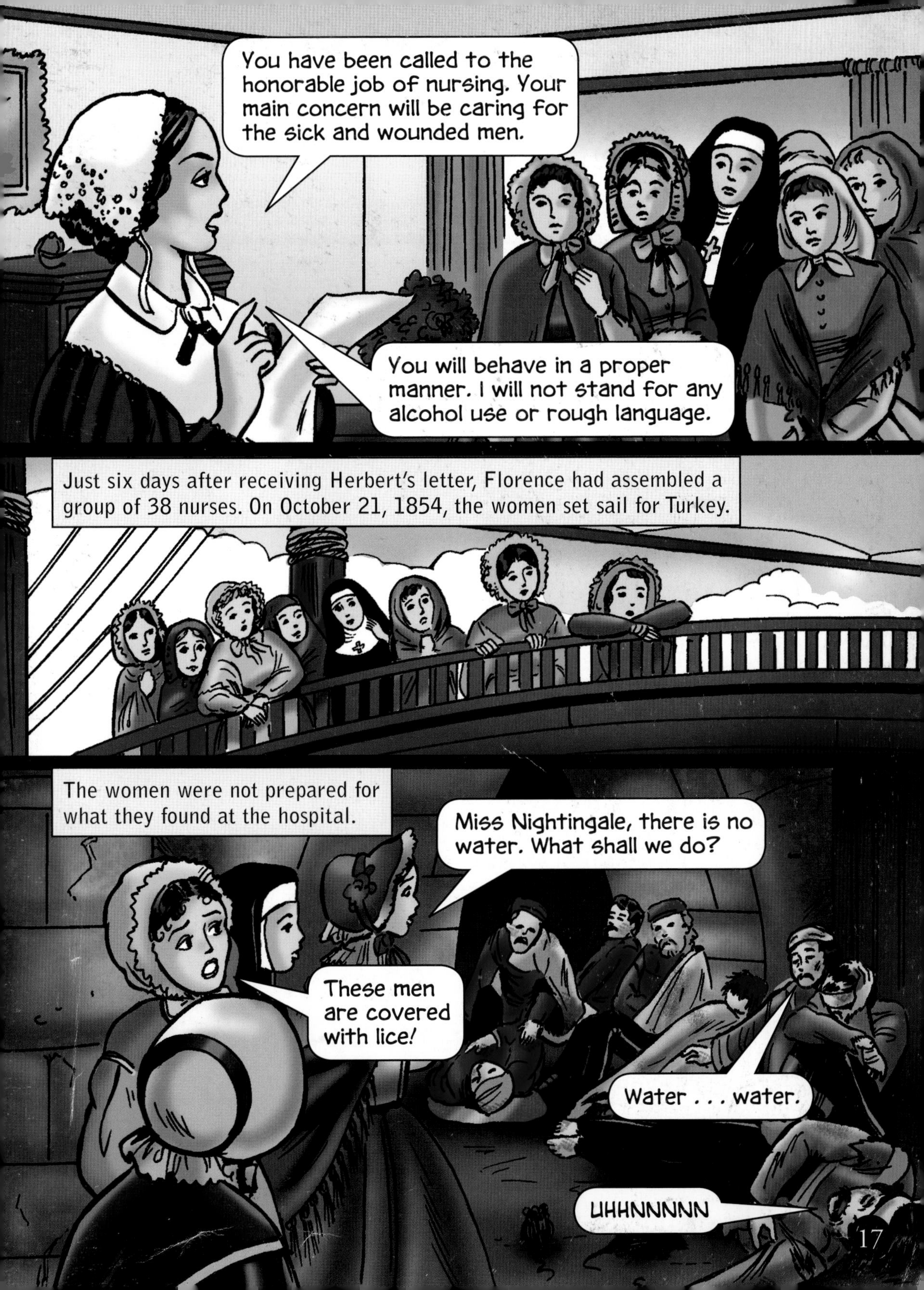
You have been called to the honorable job of nursing. Your main concern will be caring for the sick and wounded men.
You will behave in a proper manner. I will not stand for any alcohol use or rough language.
Just six days after receiving Herbert's letter, Florence had assembled a group of 38 nurses. On October 21, 1854, the women set sail for Turkey.
The women were not prepared for what they found at the hospital.
Miss Nightingale, there is no water. What shall we do?
These men are covered with lice!
Water . . . water.
UHHNNNNN

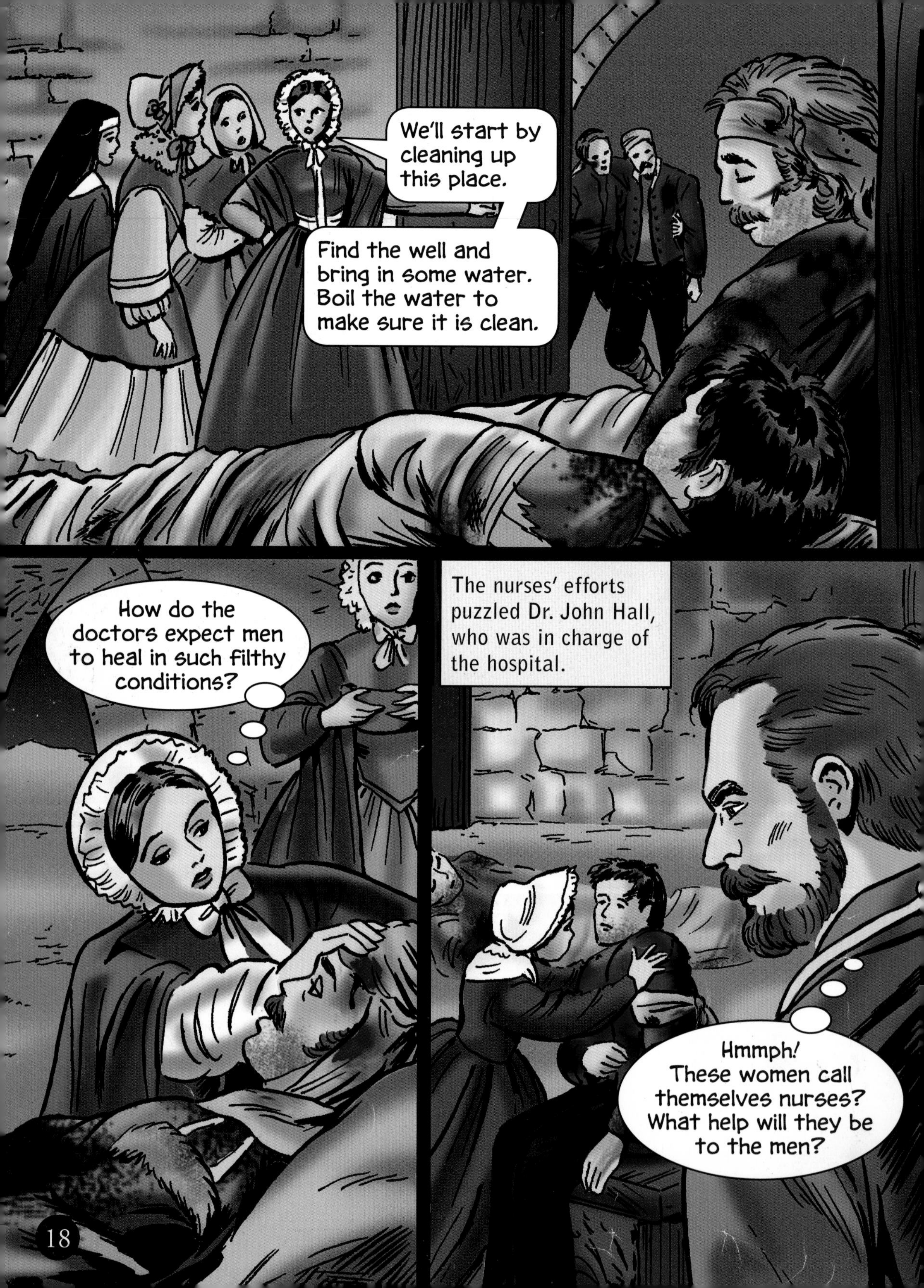

We'll start by cleaning up this place.
Find the well and bring in some water. Boil the water to make sure it is clean.
How do the doctors expect men to heal in such filthy conditions?
The nurses' efforts puzzled Dr. John Hall, who was in charge of the hospital.
Hmmph! These women call themselves nurses? What help will they be to the men?

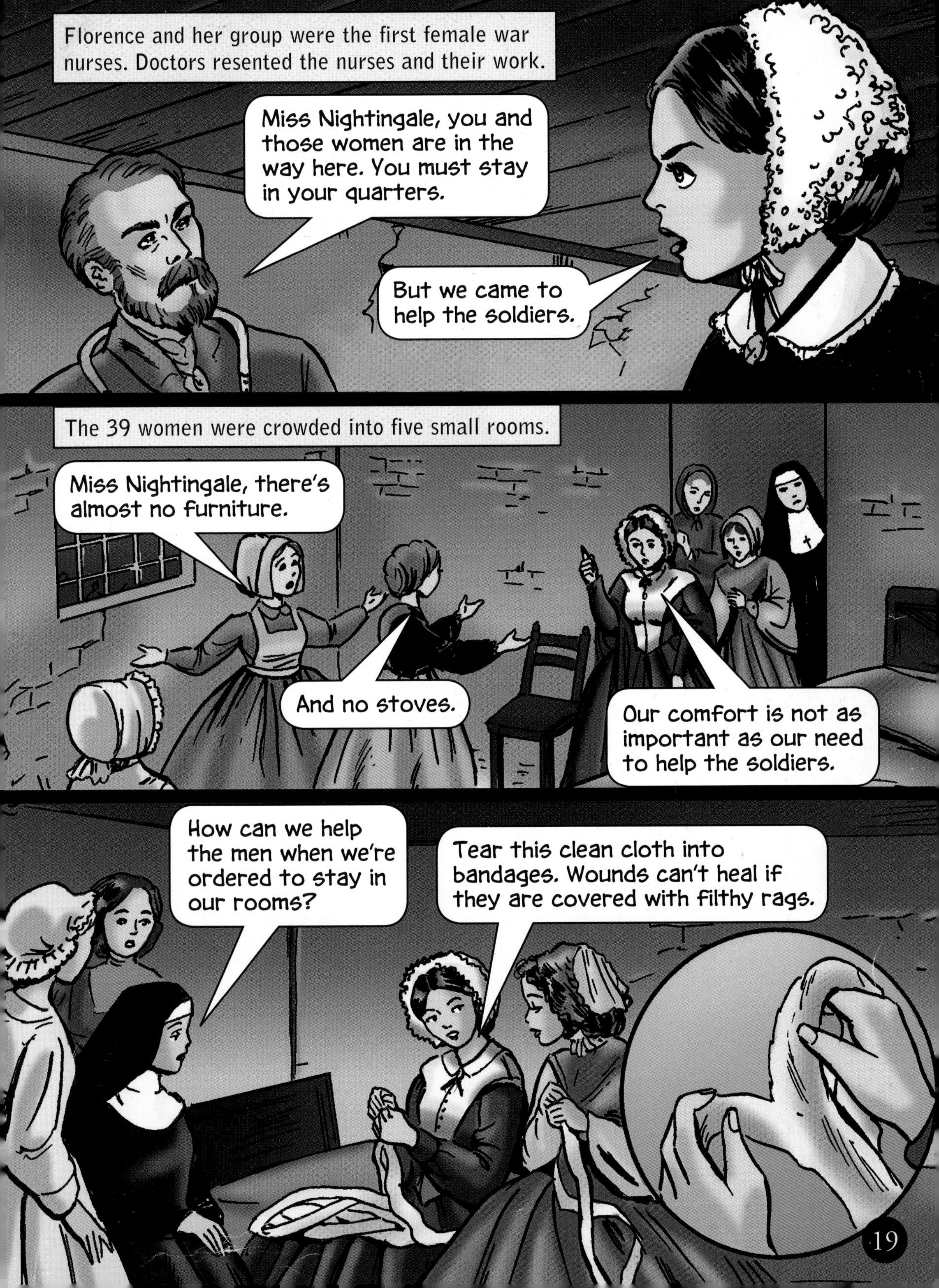
Florence and her group were the first female war nurses. Doctors resented the nurses and their work.
Miss Nightingale, you and those women are in the way here. You must stay in your quarters.
But we came to help the soldiers.
The 39 women were crowded into five small rooms.
Miss Nightingale, there's almost no furniture.
And no stoves.
Our comfort is not as important as our need to help the soldiers.
How can we help the men when we're ordered to stay in our rooms?
Tear this clean cloth into bandages. Wounds can't heal if they are covered with filthy rags.

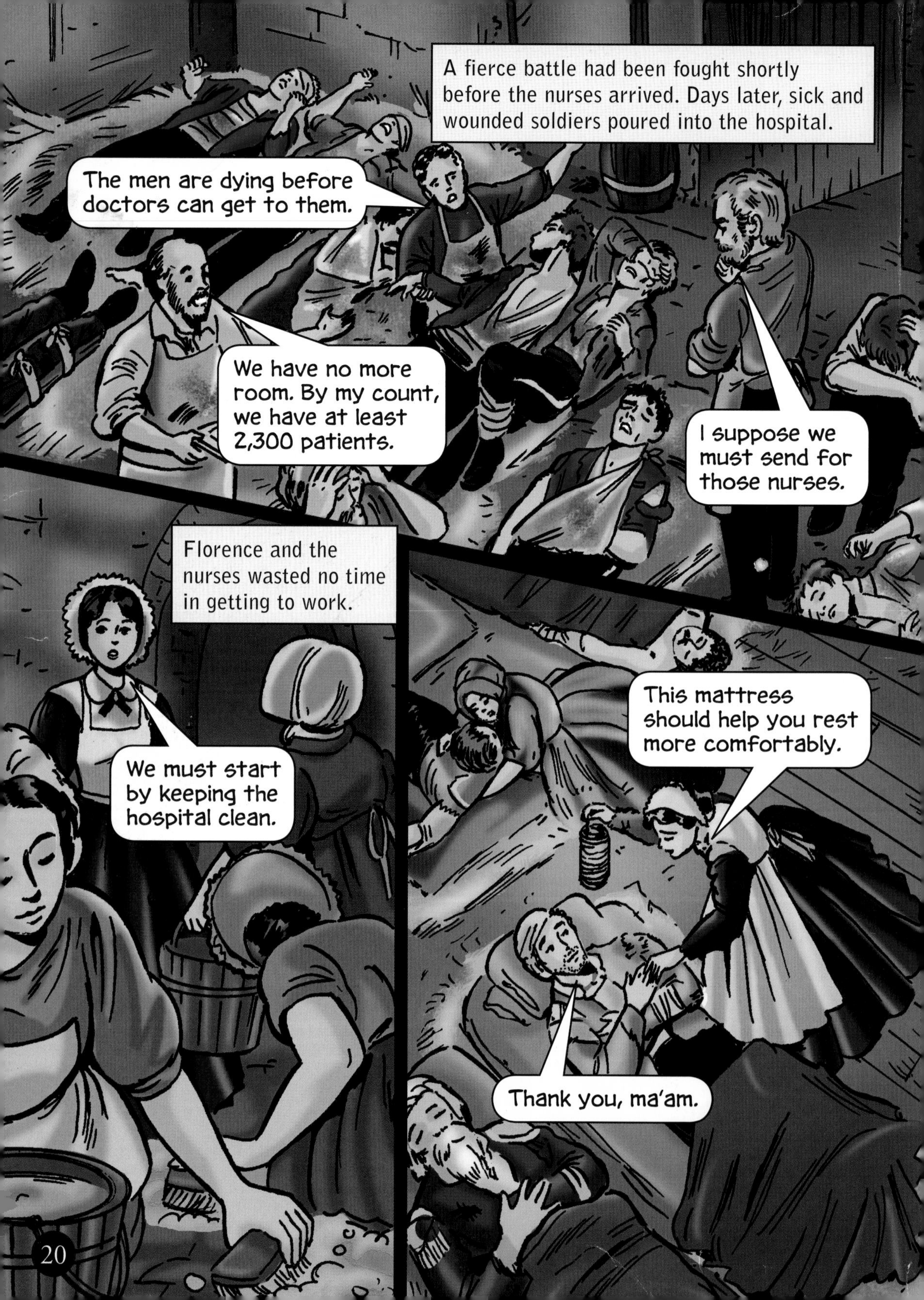

A fierce battle had been fought shortly before the nurses arrived. Days later, sick and wounded soldiers poured into the hospital.
The men are dying before doctors can get to them.
We have no more room. By my count, we have at least 2,300 patients.
I suppose we must send for those nurses.
Florence and the nurses wasted no time in getting to work.
We must start by keeping the hospital clean.
This mattress should help you rest more comfortably.
Thank you, ma'am.

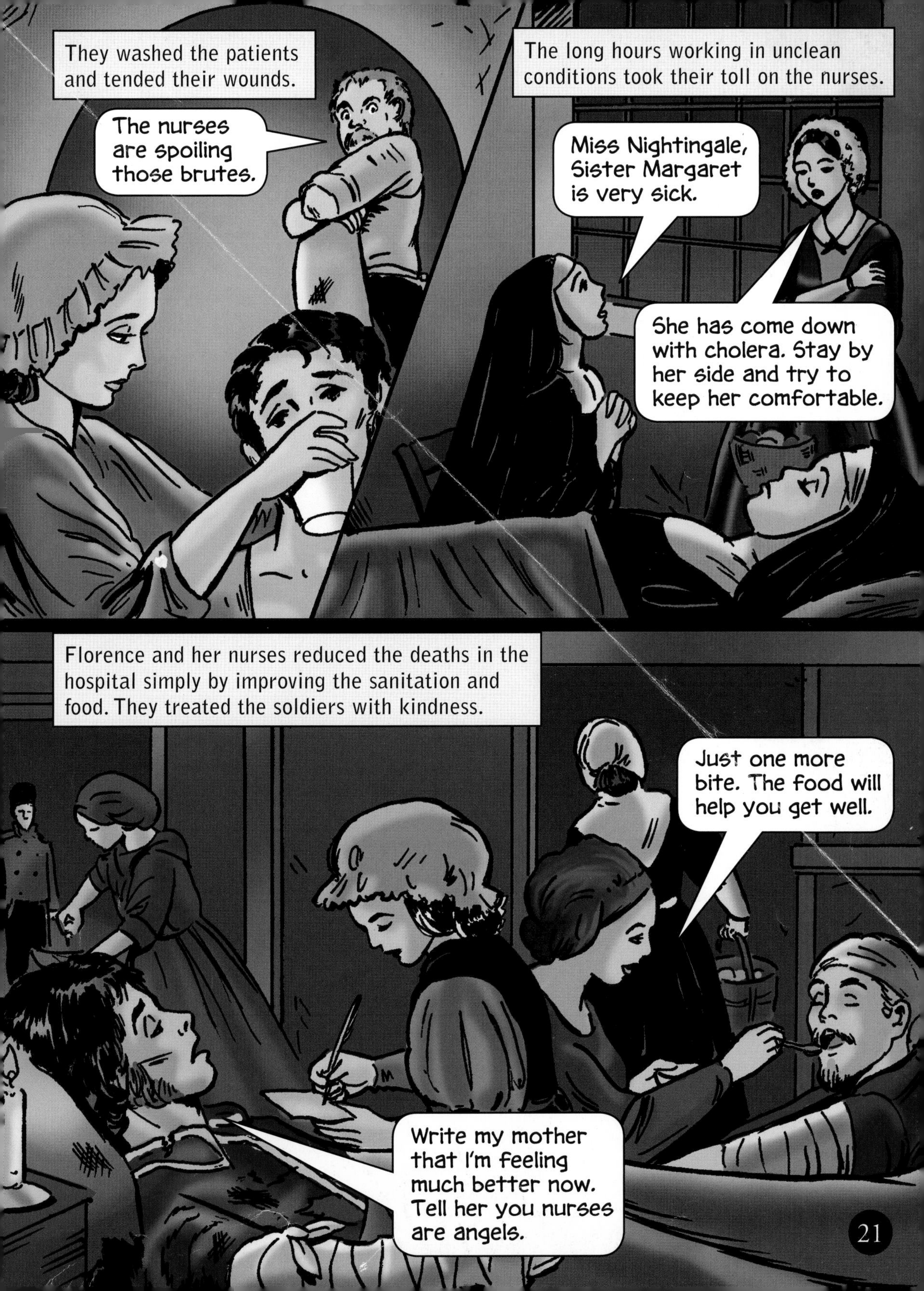
They washed the patients and tended their wounds.
The nurses are spoiling those brutes.
The long hours working in unclean conditions took their toll on the nurses.
Miss Nightingale, Sister Margaret is very sick.
She has come down with cholera. Stay by her side and try to keep her comfortable.
Florence and her nurses reduced the deaths in the hospital simply by improving the sanitation and food. They treated the soldiers with kindness.
Just one more bite. The food will help you get well.
Write my mother that I'm feeling much better now. Tell her you nurses are angels.

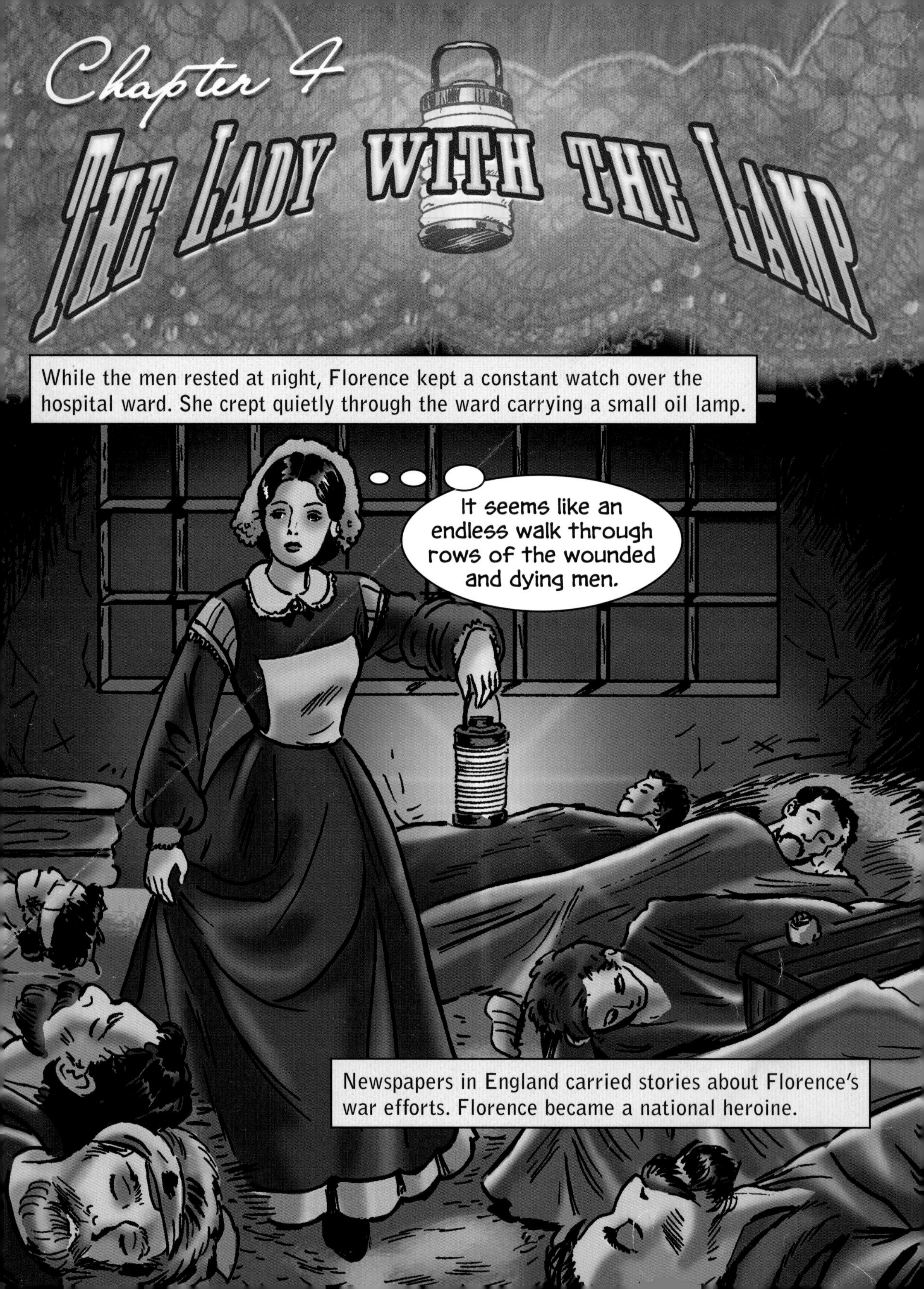
Chapter 4
THE LADY WITH THE LAMP
While the men rested at night, Florence kept a constant watch over the hospital ward. She crept quietly through the ward carrying a small oil lamp.
It seems like an endless walk through rows of the wounded and dying men.
Newspapers in England carried stories about Florence's war efforts. Florence became a national heroine.

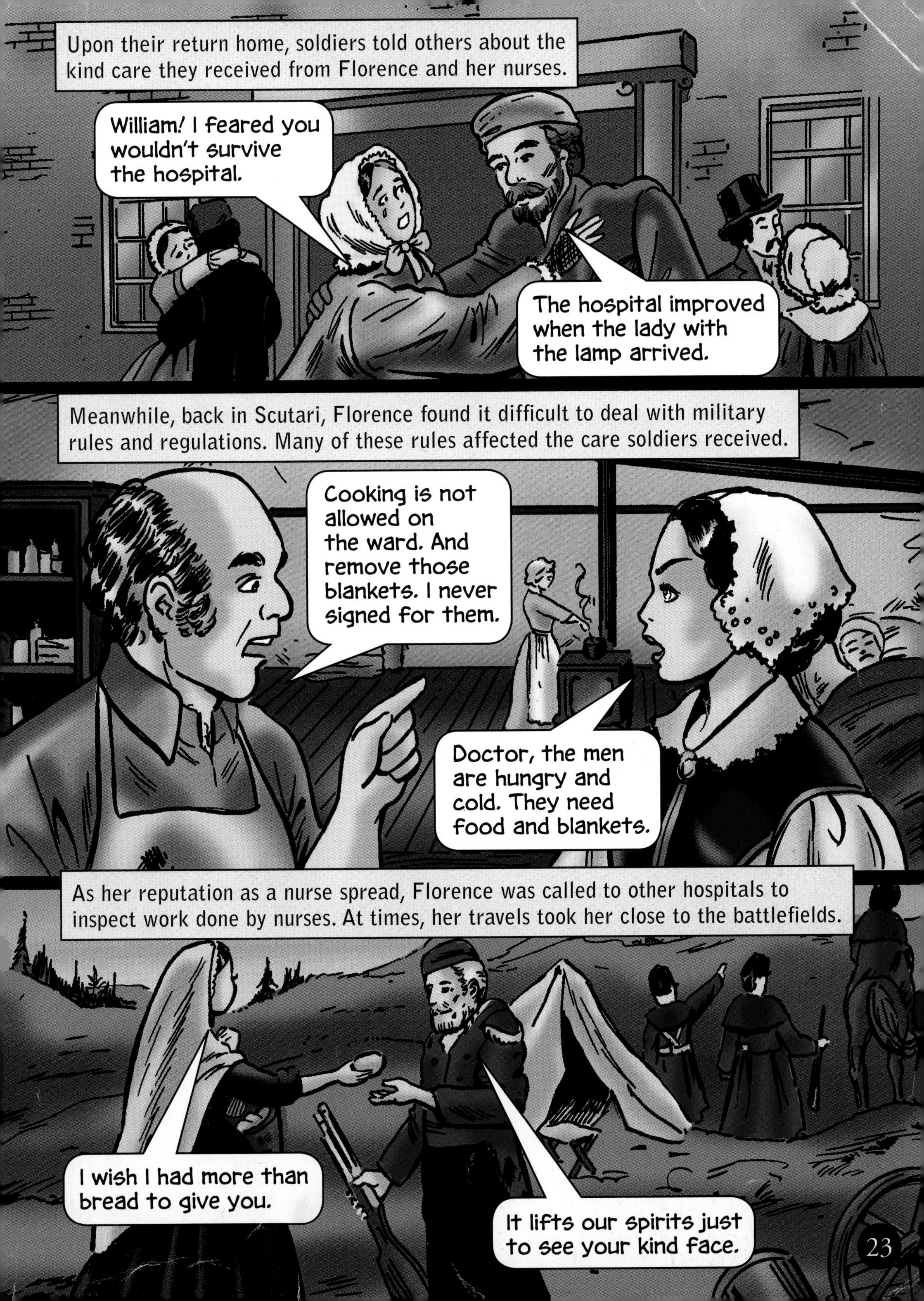
Upon their return home, soldiers told others about the kind care they received from Florence and her nurses.
William! I feared you wouldn't survive the hospital.
The hospital improved when the lady with the lamp arrived.
Meanwhile, back in Scutari, Florence found it difficult to deal with military rules and regulations. Many of these rules affected the care soldiers received.
Cooking is not allowed on the ward. And remove those blankets. I never signed for them.
Doctor, the men are hungry and cold. They need food and blankets.
As her reputation as a nurse spread, Florence was called to other hospitals to inspect work done by nurses. At times, her travels took her close to the battlefields.
I wish I had more than bread to give you.
It lifts our spirits just to see your kind face.

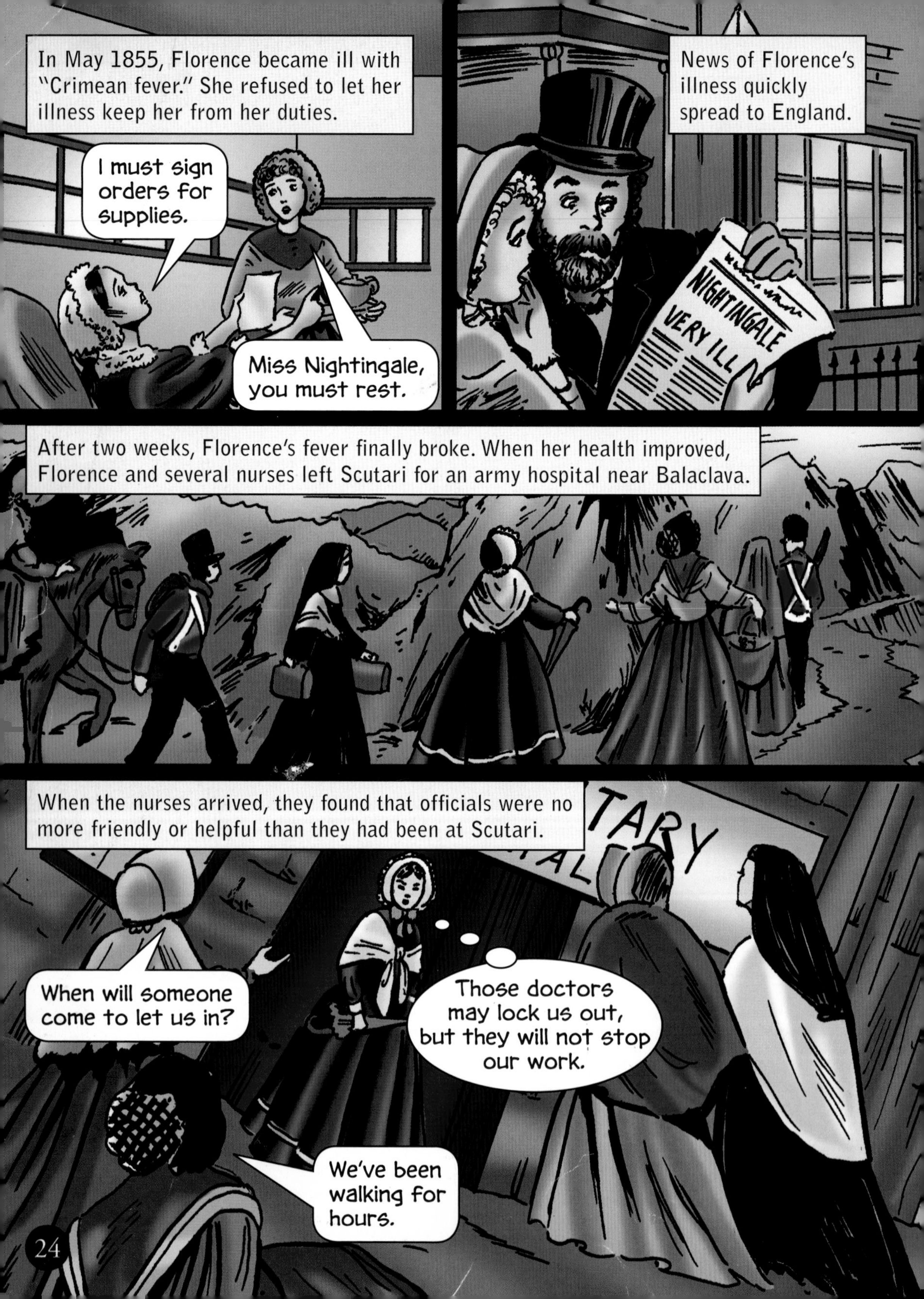
In May 1855, Florence became ill with "Crimean fever." She refused to let her illness keep her from her duties.
I must sign orders for supplies.
Miss Nightingale, you must rest.
News of Florence's illness quickly spread to England.
NIGHTINGALE VERY ILL
After two weeks, Florence's fever finally broke. When her health improved, Florence and several nurses left Scutari for an army hospital near Balaclava.
When the nurses arrived, they found that officials were no more friendly or helpful than they had been at Scutari.
TARY
When will someone come to let us in?
Those doctors may lock us out, but they will not stop our work.
We've been walking for hours.

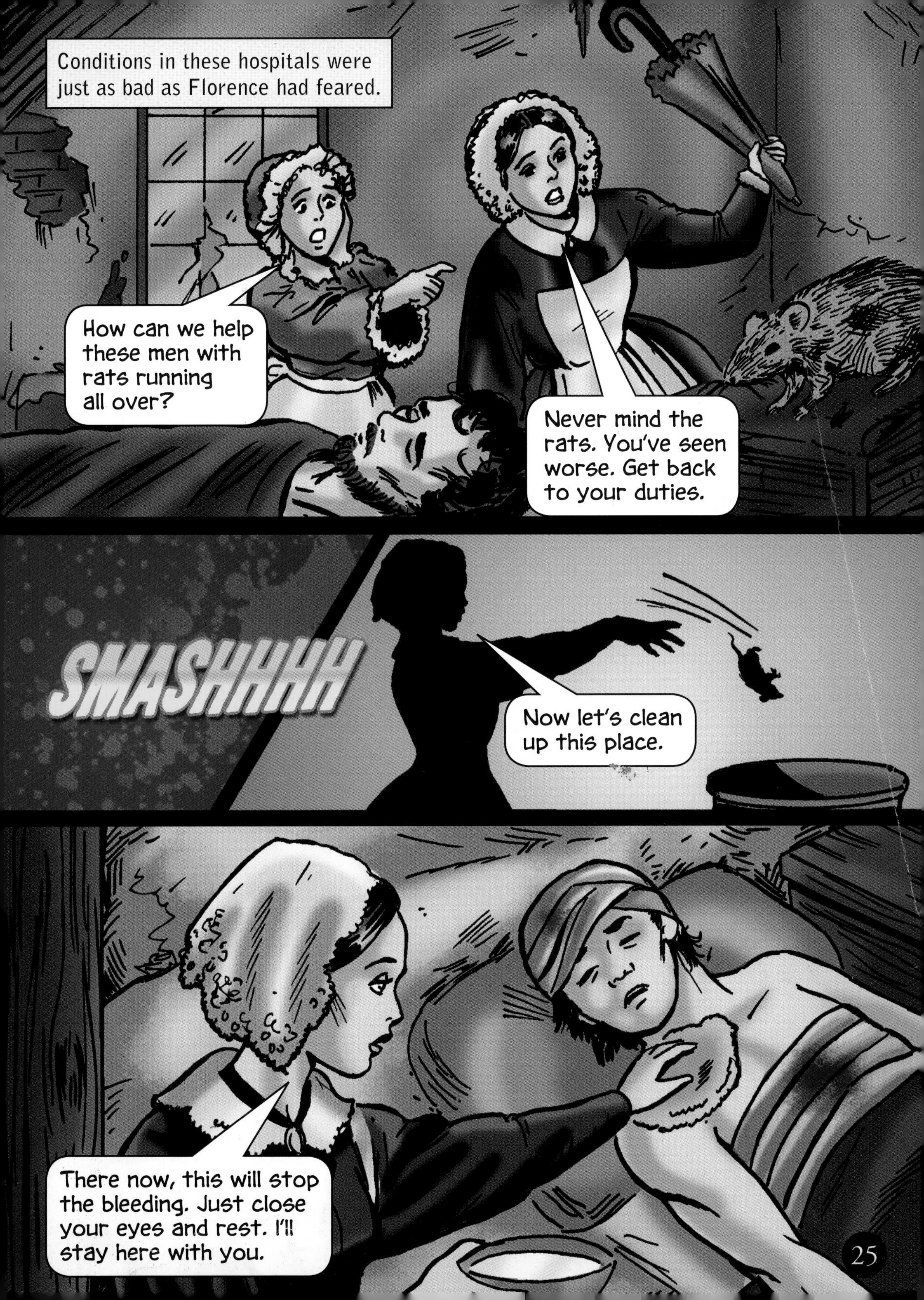
Conditions in these hospitals were just as bad as Florence had feared.
How can we help these men with rats running all over?
Never mind the rats. You've seen worse. Get back to your duties.
SMASHHHH
Now let's clean up this place.
There now, this will stop the bleeding. Just close your eyes and rest. I'll stay here with you.

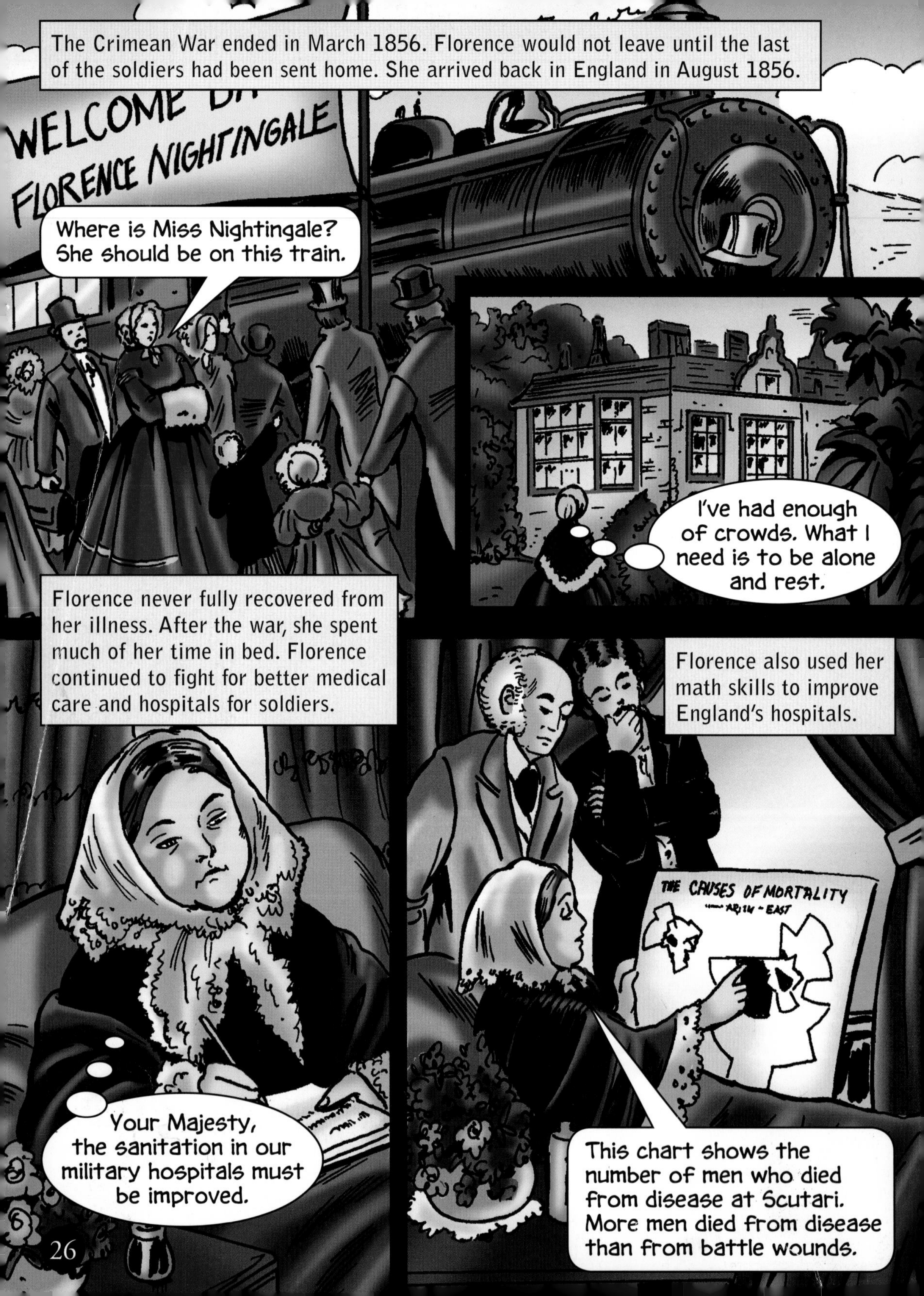
The Crimean War ended in March 1856. Florence would not leave until the last of the soldiers had been sent home. She arrived back in England in August 1856.
WELCOME BA
FLORENCE NIGHTINGALE
Where is Miss Nightingale? She should be on this train.
I've had enough of crowds. What I need is to be alone and rest.
Florence never fully recovered from her illness. After the war, she spent much of her time in bed. Florence continued to fight for better medical care and hospitals for soldiers.
Your Majesty, the sanitation in our military hospitals must be improved.
Florence also used her math skills to improve England's hospitals.
THE CAUSES OF MORTALITY
This chart shows the number of men who died from disease at Scutari. More men died from disease than from battle wounds.

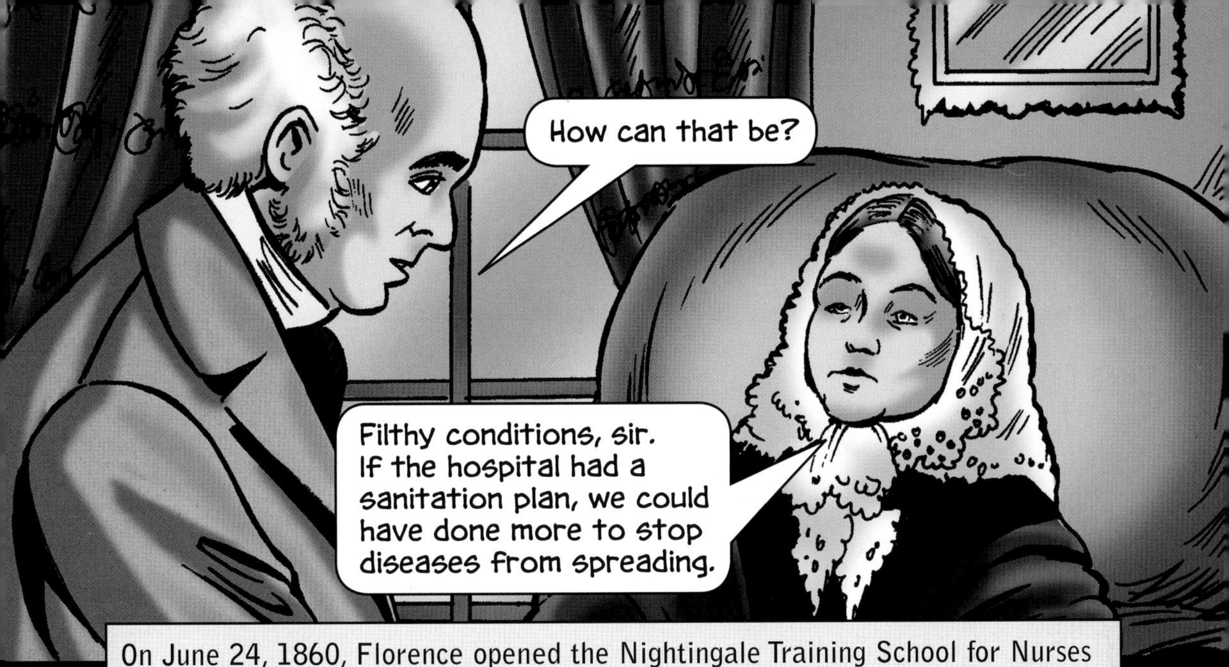
How can that be?
Filthy conditions, sir. If the hospital had a sanitation plan, we could have done more to stop diseases from spreading.
On June 24, 1860, Florence opened the Nightingale Training School for Nurses at St. Thomas' Hospital in London. When Nightingale students graduated, they became certified nurses. Nightingale nurses worked at hospitals across England.

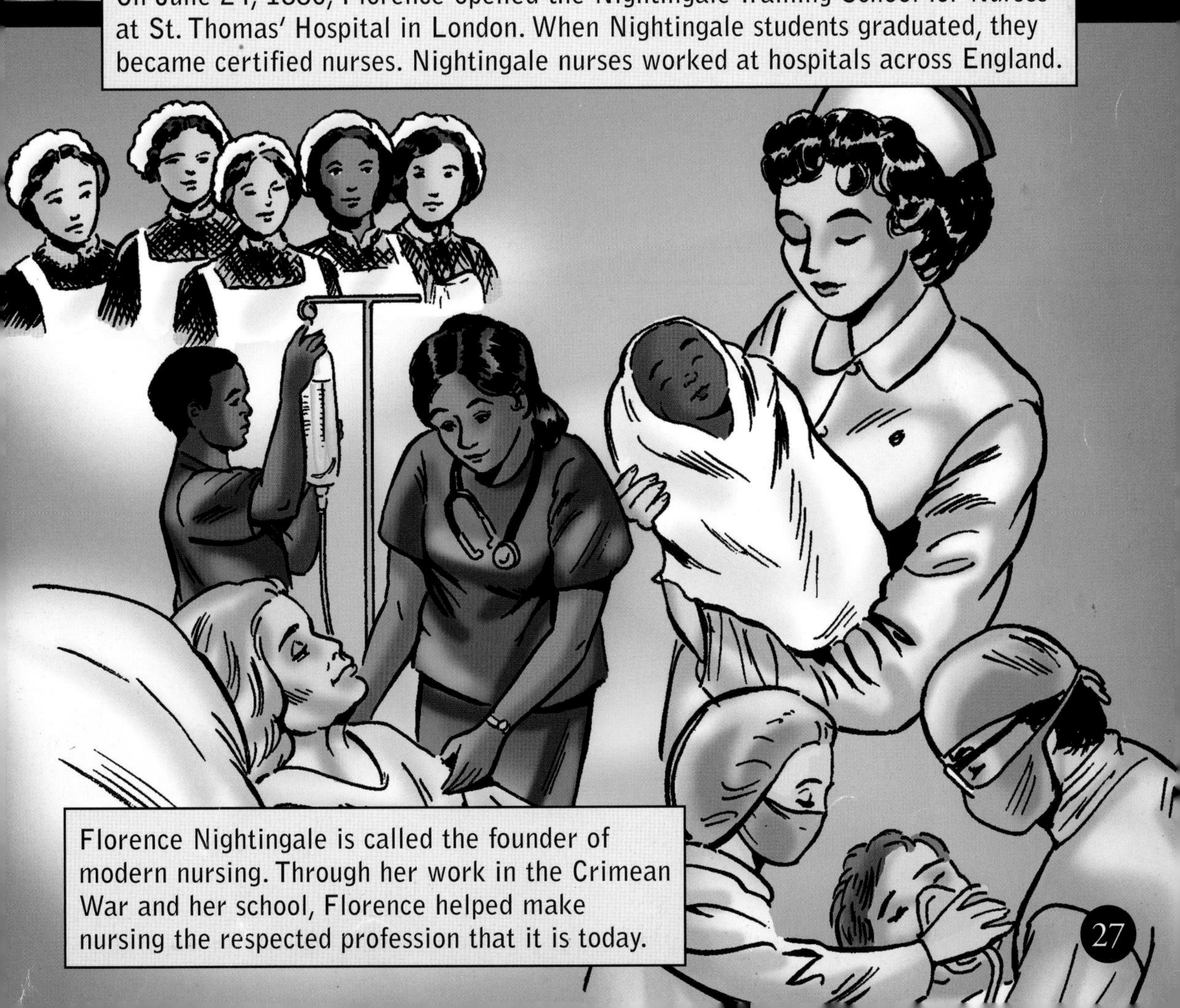
Florence Nightingale is called the founder of modern nursing. Through her work in the Crimean War and her school, Florence helped make nursing the respected profession that it is today.

MORE ABOUT FLORENCE NIGHTINGALE

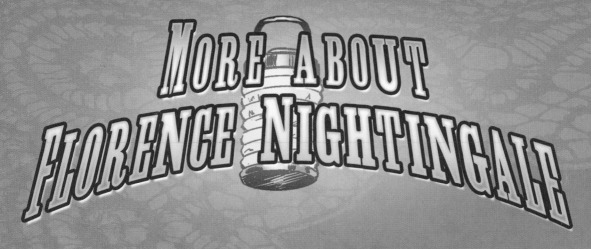

- Florence Nightingale was born May 12, 1820, in Florence, Italy. Her parents named her after the city where she was born. On August 13, 1910, Florence died at age 90 in London, England.

- Florence became one of the most famous women in Europe. Poems, books, and songs were written about her. Florence also had a street, racehorse, and lifeboat named in her honor.

- Historians believe that the "Crimean fever" that Florence came down with might have been typhus or brucellosis. Both illnesses cause high fever.

- Florence received many medals for her outstanding work. In 1883, Queen Victoria awarded her the Royal Red Cross. In 1907, King Edward VII gave Florence the Order of Merit. Florence was the first woman to receive that medal.

- Florence published many books and pamphlets on hospitals, nursing, and the importance of sanitation. Her book *Notes on Nursing* sold 15,000 copies in one month and is still in print today.

Florence was the first woman elected as an honorary member of the American Statistical Association. Her ability to use statistics to show the effect of unsanitary hospital conditions earned her this honor.

 In 1861, Florence helped the U.S. government set up military hospitals during the Civil War (1861–1865).

 When Florence died, England's King Edward VII offered to have her buried in Westminster Abbey, where England's kings and heroes are buried. Instead, Florence was buried at St. Margaret's Church, in East Wellow, Hampshire. Florence had wanted a small funeral, but the churchyard at St. Margaret's was packed with people, many of them old soldiers in their uniforms.

 As a tribute to Florence, Lystra E. Gretter of the Farrand Training School for Nurses in Detroit, Michigan, wrote the Florence Nightingale Pledge in 1893. This pledge is still said at graduation ceremonies and other events honoring nurses.

GLOSSARY

cholera (KOL-ur-uh)—a disease that causes sickness and diarrhea

disgrace (diss-GRAYSS)—a reaction of shame or disapproval from others

heroine (HER-oh-uhn)—a girl or woman who shows strength and courage by doing a good thing

reputation (rep-yuh-TAY-shuhn)—your worth or character, as judged by other people

resign (ri-ZINE)—to give up a job or position voluntarily

respectable (ri-SPEK-tuh-buhl)—to behave in an honest and decent manner

sanitation (san-uh-TAY-shuhn)—to protect people from dirt and disease

INTERNET SITES

FactHound offers a safe, fun way to find Internet sites related to this book. All of the sites on FactHound have been researched by our staff.

Here's how:
1. Visit *www.facthound.com*
2. Choose your grade level.
3. Type in this book ID **073686850X** for age-appropriate sites. You may also browse subjects by clicking on letters, or by clicking on pictures and words.
4. Click on the **Fetch It** button.

FactHound will fetch the best sites for you!

READ MORE

Barnham, Kay. *Florence Nightingale: The Lady of the Lamp.* Austin, Texas: Raintree Steck-Vaughn, 2002.

Davis, Marc. *Florence Nightingale: Founder of the Nightingale School of Nursing.* Our People. Chanhassen, Minn.: Child's World, 2004.

Hinman, Bonnie. *Florence Nightingale and the Advancement of Nursing.* Uncharted, Unexplored, and Unexplained. Hockessin, Del.: Mitchell Lane, 2005.

Lynch, Emma. *Florence Nightingale.* Lives and Times. Chicago: Heinemann, 2005.

BIBLIOGRAPHY

Dossey, Barbara Montgomery. *Florence Nightingale: Mystic, Visionary, Healer.* Springhouse, Pa.: Springhouse Corporation, 2000.

Nightingale, Florence. *I Have Done My Duty: Florence Nightingale in the Crimean War, 1854–1856.* Iowa City, Iowa: University of Iowa Press, 1987.

Nightingale, Florence. *Notes on Nursing: What It Is and What It Is Not.* Philadelphia: University of Pennsylvania Printing Office, 1965.

INDEX